Bird in My Hand

BIRD
IN MY
HAND

Loraine Hodgkinson

'Sparrows in the Wild'
by Chris Mead

WHITTET BOOKS

First published 1987
Bird in My Hand © 1987 by Loraine Hodgkinson
Sparrows in the Wild © 1987 by Chris Mead
Whittet Books Ltd, 18 Anley Road, London W14 0BY

Design by Paul Minns

British Library Cataloguing in Publication Data

Hodgkinson, Loraine
Bird in my hand.
1. English sparrow
I. Title   II. Mead, Chris. Sparrows in
the wild
598.8'83   QL696.P264

ISBN 0-905483-56-1

The photographs that appear between pp 64 and 65
were taken by the author. The author and publishers
are grateful to the following for permission to
reproduce the photographs whose numbers appear in
brackets after their names: Ernie Janes (1, 9, 10, 11, 13,
15); Chris Mead (12); Mike Wilkes (4, 5, 6, 16); Roger
Wilmshurst (2, 3, 7, 8, 14).

Typeset by Inforum Ltd, Portsmouth
Printed and bound by The Bath Press

Contents

1 To Kill or not to Kill?   7
2 The First Feed   10
3 Plans   12
4 Bimbo/Robbie   14
5 The Muntjacs   19
6 The Dingly-Danglies   25
7 The Bird-Seed Buyer and the Art Show   28
8 E.T.'s Narrow Escape   32
9 Travelling Birds   35
10 Pangs of Guilt and an Interesting Discovery   39
11 The Bumble Bee Nest   42
12 To the Vet   45
13 Difficult Days   51
14 A Stupid Accident   54
15 Froghoppers   59
16 A Turning Point   63
17 Lake Garda   65
18 Some Precedents   70
19 The Sick Bay   75
20 A Very Handsome Bird   81
21 The Eavesdropper   84
22 Family Life   89
Epilogue   90

SPARROWS IN THE WILD *by Chris Mead*

Sparrows in the Wild   103
What is a House Sparrow?   105
The Extent of Sparrowdom   107
The Sparrow Year   115
And So Into the Outside World   126

1

To Kill or not to Kill?

The urgent scream of my daughter brought me racing up from the kitchen garden, knee pads dropping to my ankles, trowel still in hand. Burglar? Rapist? Peeping Tom? Now, looking back, I wonder: what if I had been out on that particular June morning? What if Gemma had not been sunbathing on the terrace at that particular spot? I know that I would have been saved a great deal of worry, heartache and some sleepless nights. I also know that the joy and sense of privilege has outweighed all that and my life has been altered and enriched. What was this momentous event which so startled my daughter and brought out the latent lioness in me?

'Something fell off the roof and nearly hit *me*,' said Gemma indignantly, 'it went splat onto the ground over there.'

She popped a chocolate into her mouth, closed her eyes and lay back on the sun lounger. There, on the York stone terrace, wriggled a tiny, naked and blind baby sparrow. *Passer domesticus*. Not all babies are beautiful; this one resembled a very small skinned frog. I had seen them before. Each spring there were pathetic little rigor-mortised bodies on the terrace or lawn which I hastily popped into the compost heap before the dog should find them. What stupid sparrow parents to persist in building such a manifestly unsuccessful nest each year in the angle of a dormer window and the roof.

This time it was unpleasant. Not cold. Not dead. Humane despatch? Squeeze its tiny bony neck? Put it on the drive and reverse the car over it? Drop it in a bucket of water, or, simpler, just tread on it? We had buried the hamster that very morning by a lily in the front garden. I really had no choice.

'What did we do with the unused hamster bedding, Gemma?'

As I examined the tiny livid body for damage, I knew that I was committing all my time for at least the next three weeks. It would be cruel to play at keeping it alive for a few agonizing days. I was going to have to make a proper job of rearing it and feeding it as its parents would have fed it. But how would they? Although I like watching birds, I have never kept a caged bird or believed in taming wild ones.

When I was about eight years old, my friend and I bought a day-old chick each from Enfield market. I naturally chose the runt of the brood, a small, cowering, brown thing. The rest were noisy, piping, fluffy cream chicks. My friend's bird died quite soon, but mine grew to be a fine black cockerel – the terror of the neighbourhood. I remember that it lived in my buttoned-up cardigan during the day and on a hot-water bottle under a mop-head in a box with a ticking clock at night. I fed it on chopped hard-boiled egg which it pecked up by itself.

Sparrows are finches (Weaver finches & family *Ploceidae*) and notoriously difficult, as I was soon to discover. This little wriggling scrap of life had thrust itself into my care. I would certainly do my best, but I was quite ignorant and unqualified for such a task. The cockerel episode was over forty years ago . . .

Well, little squeaking thing, after that fall you must be a survivor. I can surely spare the next three weeks of my life. Even if it takes a month.

Back on the terrace I put the seemingly uninjured bird in a cosy nest in a 3″ flowerpot which I placed in a basket and tied to a pillar of the loggia. Thus, it was in the direct flight path of the parents and out of the reach of the dog. I decided to leave it for one hour and hope that those jerry-builder sparrows would see where their duty lay. During that hour I was very busy collecting greenfly. Several hundred mashed up make a heap the size of a pea. I made a substitute beak from a twig the size of a thin pencil with a smooth rounded end, then I frantically racked my brains for any dormant knowledge that would help me now. Sparrows were seed eaters and crocus destroyers. I knew that to

8

my cost in black cotton. The soft wide yellow mouth of this baby did not look as if it could cope with a petunia seed let alone a grass seed. I had seen parent sparrows hastening to nests with moth wings protruding from their bills, hadn't I? All the clever close-up pictures on film of various species of parent birds at the nest always seemed to show them stuffing newly caught living creatures down their offsprings' throats. Creepy-crawly things. Protein. Not nuts or fruit or chunks of bread which as adults I knew they ate.

I kept remembering a detail from a book written by a prisoner who reared birds in his cell: the nestlings always died after a few days until he discovered that they must have earth in their diet. Was it *The Birdman of Alcatraz* or something nearer home? Wormwood Scrubs? No, that was for prisoners on remand and I had this clear mental picture of the man scraping the dust from his cell floor and mixing it in bits of porridge. Broadmoor perhaps? Anyway, it seemed to me a logical thing to do. When preparing pheasants or chickens for the oven I cut open the gizzard to remove the contents and have often been astonished at the large amount of stones and grit therein. A nestling with a body the size of a grape would only have a pip of a gizzard and dust brought in on the shoes of the prison guards would be quite sufficient for its proper function. My substitute cell dust would be ground-up worm-casts. What else, what else? The hour was nearly up. I only had negative thoughts left. No bread – swells up inside. Besides, bread was not usually thrown out to birds in summer. No tinned baby food. It must be as natural as possible. Come on, *think*. The poor bird will not survive on worm-casts and sympathy alone.

There was a lot of screeching still going on up in the roof but the returning parents were carrying nothing visible to me anxiously watching from below. They were also totally ignoring their newly hatched offspring in the substitute nest. I wished my little cast-out would screech and open its mouth as they flew over. Why was it so silent? Was it dying of cold, shock, hunger?

9

Three-quarters of an hour had gone by and I could wait no longer. I fetched the ladder and at twelve noon on Tuesday June 26th, 1984, took up my duties as foster mother.

2

The First Feed

From the first I decided to keep a note of what food I administered and at what time, so that I would be able to tell which food agreed with the bird and which, if any, had an adverse effect. Also, I thought, if I varied the food as much as possible there would be less chance of inadvertently poisoning my charge.

My first notes read: *Prized open mouth and rammed in greenfly. Drank water avidly.* How clumsy I was. Over-anxious and unnerved by the screeching emanating from the huge gape waving about on top of the disproportionately long neck. Just as I managed to balance a clump of greenfly on my twig, the bird decided to close its mouth. By the time I had levered it open again the clump of greenfly had mysteriously come to life and was dispersing rapidly up the stick, into the bedding, over my hands and onto the ground.

If at first you don't succeed, go in for firmer methods. So I killed the remaining dinner and smeared it onto the very end of the stick. Then I grasped the squirming nestling's body, with its flailing half-inch boomerang-shaped wings and miniature scrabbling drumsticks, firmly in my left fist, allowing only the top-heavy head to protrude. This also supported the neck which when fully extended and screeching for food was as long as the body. Feeding became easier as soon as I realized that the stick had to be pushed down the throat and neck for almost an inch. It reminded me of sword swallowers and I winced as I did it but the bird seemed quite happy with the method. The water I put into my own mouth first, closed my lips over the beak and transferred the water forcibly. The Squeaker obviously enjoyed this and started sucking strongly for more.

As soon as I had gathered enough greenfly again, I repeated the procedure and was inordinately pleased that nourishment was going down and staying down. When the semi-transparent nether-end was heaved over the edge of the nest and a normal-looking chick dropping emerged, I was quite proud.

Soon my roses and Indian balsam were all relieved of their aphids and I cast around desperately for caterpillars. This year there had been a dearth of caterpillars. Not one on my spring greens and hardly any on the roses. I was looking forward to showing off my unblemished fruit, flowers and vegetables in the local flower show in two weeks' time.

Then I spotted the cuckoo-spit on the lavender. Of course! The little froghoppers make it to protect their *soft bodies* from birds. I soon had a dozen or so out of their bubble baths and into my little plastic box. They went down the squeaking gape a treat; before you could say 'sword' in fact.

My mother grew lavender and she lived just round the corner. Clasping my empty plastic box, I raced round the corner and down the hill.

'A cup of tea, dear?'

'No, I must have froghoppers. You see, it's this baby bird . . .'

'Well, I think it's very cruel. You'll never rear it. I don't hold with keeping a wild thing in captivity. It's unnatural. The other birds won't accept it. Besides, it won't live that long.'

'It's not. I will. They will. It *will*. Ta, must fly!' Panting back up the hill, my head full of ethical problems, a box full of froghoppers and my stomach beginning to rumble, I thought I'd treat myself to a cup of tea and some deep thinking.

As I tiptoed past the sleeping foster baby, I saw that my lethargic human offspring had managed to drag her sun lounger onto the lawn and was fast asleep in the sun.

To my utter horror, there, on the vacated York stone terrace, lay the still body of a tiny newly hatched baby sparrow. *Passer domesticus!*

3

Plans

It was of course déjà vu. Please let it be. But it wasn't, and I scooped up the pale cool body and breathed my tea-warmed breath into my enfolding hand until I felt a stirring and saw a warm pinkness suffuse my new charge. But how many more? I thought I could just about cope with one; but two, three? A whole nestful?

Moral dilemma: where does one draw the line? I must obviously draw the line when I feel that the lives of the few are in jeopardy for the sake of a gamble that I can rear a whole brood. I knew that with only two hands, two birds were my limit. That was the theory anyway. Thankfully I was never put to the test. All was very quiet up on the roof and I soon realized that there were no cheeping nestlings left.

With the arrival of E.T. (well, it did look remarkably like a scaled-down version of that currently popular space alien), I felt a vague resentment on behalf of the original Squeaker. Instead of having my complete and undivided attention, it was going to have to share. I would just have to work twice as hard. Against that, however, the company and body warmth of its sibling were a positive benefit.

I think I must have been muttering to myself or even shouting aloud imprecations at those profligate parents up on the roof, because Gemma awoke sufficiently to turn over on the sun lounger.

'I *thought* I heard a lot of squeaking. Actually, I thought I saw an adult fluttering down.' More about that later.

'Coo-ee! Lorr-rraine!' My French friend Yveline from next-door-but-one. How fortuitous. Her long, beautifully manicured red fingernails were just the tools I needed for reluctant beaks.

'Yveline, look what I've got!'

Midst Oos and Ah, the poor darlings, I repeated the story.

'But of course they will live. But of course I will help.' That 'But of course . . .', varied occasionally by 'Naturally . . .', which was always followed by practical help and what seemed to me wild optimism, was such a comfort and prop in the days and weeks that followed.

We sat on the stone wall of the rockery feeding the birds and discussing ways and means. The first priority was to obtain the next meal; within the next hour preferably.

I once read of a researcher who counted the number of visits a pair of great tits made to their nest whilst feeding their young. It was thousands not hundreds. I was impressed at the time, but how much more was I impressed now that it had a personal relevance. No wonder balding, bare-necked and wild-eyed adult birds were such a common sight in July. Fancy raising two broods of up to ten screaming chicks. It was the robins and blackbirds that seemed the most bedraggled, though. I can't recall seeing a harassed-looking sparrow. Actually, they are not the sort of bird one notices. 'Quick everybody, there is a sparrow!' No, they are always there – part of the roof and lawn furniture.

As I only had two nestlings not ten and as I was a human being with intelligent independent thought and therefore cap-able of producing larger quantities of food than mere bird-brains, I could leave the gaps between feeds longer. Birds all quietened down after dark but were up with the sun. Well, mine were young enough to be trained from the start. They must sleep when I slept and that was that. If I fed them way past their natural bedtime they would be more inclined to lie in. At least until 7 a.m.?

The one huge snag with the first of these premises was that although I was a big grown-up human capable of procuring food, I was not clever enough to know what food to procure. It would have to be trial and error. I had often watched blackbirds' beaks adribble with small worms dashing to their nests as soon

13

as the eggs were hatched and tits with small caterpillars but I could not recall ever actually seeing a sparrow's nest, let alone *Passer domesticus* in a parental role. Squeaker and E.T.'s parents were even now dancing on the gutter edge, making short aimless flights, preening and generally amusing themselves.

'Yveline, do you think we could get hold of those revolting little white maggots fishermen use?'

'But of course, I will go first thing tomorrow to the pet shops of Potters Bar.'

'And I will go first thing to the library in the village and look up Sparrow in all the suitable books. I'll also ask around in case anybody knows anybody who is an expert or knows an expert.''

Feeling we had made some headway I despatched Yveline to scour her nasturtiums and, taking up my little plastic box, I called 'Walkies!' to the dog and headed for the woods.

I was very lucky: just inside the entrance to the woods I saw blob after blob of cuckoo-spit adorning blackberry bushes, honeysuckle and even the grass. I soon evolved a brisk routine: with thumb and forefinger dive into the spit, grasp the froghopper, blow off the bubbles, tap my finger with the adhering insect sharply onto the edge of the container, pop back the lid and wipe finger and thumb on shorts ready for the next foray. Dive, blow, tap, snap, wipe. Dive, blow, tap, snap, wipe. In ten minutes I had a box full and the perplexed dog was called back after the shortest 'walkie' it had ever had. I also remembered that 'the Master' was due home soon and I must prepare a more substantial repast for the human members of the family.

4

Bimbo/Robbie

At this juncture I must introduce our dog Bimbo. Ten years ago we moved back to this district where I was brought up. My eldest daughter, Lois, was two years into her teens and not too keen on a change of stamping ground. Gemma was eleven. Extolling the virtues of our new home I explained that, as Nana and Grandad were just around the corner, we could keep a dog as they would look after it when we went on holidays.

By some strange mismanagement we were due to go to Spain shortly after moving in. However, as soon as we were settled back again we would go to the local dogs' home. Thus with the sounds of the current favourite Spanish pop group, El Bimbo, barely faded from our ears, we presented ourselves at the R.S.P.C.A. Southridge Animal Centre.

Not an exercise to be recommended to the merely curious. We were told that as it was too near Christmas we would not be allowed to select a puppy. This is a sensible precaution with which I heartily concur. What a sad sight it was touring the pens and seeing 'man's best friend' cast off and rejected. However uncaring the owner, to a dog, he is god. The dog cannot understand his abandonment.

I stopped in astonishment in front of a beautiful Afghan hound sitting in dignified aloofness in the centre of his pen. Why on earth was *he* here? Was he lost?

'This one has had three homes but he is untrainable and incontinent,' said the kennel girl.

Looking at the rest it was not too hard to see that they were rejects. As puppies I suppose they might have had some charm but as they grew and ate more, grew and wanted more exercise, and grew and became large and unattractive, it was easy to see why for financial or spatial reasons these dogs had to go rather than the telly. It is also a sad statistic that just before the holiday season many more family pets are abandoned than at any other time. Dogs and cats are often found on motorways having been thrown from cars. What is the thinking behind that? Kill a few people in a possible multiple pile-up in preference to taking the trouble of finding the unfortunate creature a new home or have it put to sleep? Out of sight, out of mind, I suppose. As for the cringing victims of cruelty, dear oh dear! No, an animal rescue centre is not the place to go if you want to think well of your fellow men.

The children were plainly disappointed we could not have a puppy but I had already seen the one for us. Sharing a pen with a black overlarge Spaniel type with scummy eyes, was an eager, smallish, longish haired, multi-coloured and multi-variety dog. I read the card with its particulars: 'Female. Name – Robbie. House trained. Good with children. Good traveller.'

'Why don't you put it on a lead and run round the paddock with it to see how you get on together?' suggested the kennel girl.

I could not wait to get it away from poor old scummy eyes in case it was catching. The little dog's prancing delight with our company was mutual; at least with me. The potential master was doom-laden as usual.

'If you have it, you take full responsibility. It'll ruin the garden, destroy the furniture and you'll soon get fed up with taking it out in the rain when the novelty has worn off.'

As I picked up the excited dog and hugged it, it licked my face and I murmured endearments to calm it down.

'El Bimbo, Bimbo, Jolly little Bimbo. I'll call you Bimbo.'

'Its name is Robbie. It says so on the card. I shall call it Robbie,' said Lois. And so she does to this day.

Apart from Bimbo/Robbie being a bitch and about one year old, the other particulars on the card were over optimistic. The four-mile journey home in the car put paid to the 'good traveller' bit straight away. We assumed the terror and vomiting were caused by all the stressful changes she was experiencing. Not so. For years after her stress had gone, our journeys to Norfolk in the summer were a nightmare. The terror part is cured now as I persistently took her for four-hundred-yard drives round the corner to my parents' house where the pleasure of arrival – fond greetings, tit-bits, etc. – eventually outweighed the dread of the journey being once again the preliminary to abandonment.

'House trained.' Well, the living room carpets seemed to her to be as good a place as any for answering the calls of nature. She did not know what grass and a garden were and was terrified in the woods. This was not surprising as she had come from a high-rise block of flats in the City of London. With the aid of squares of chocolate I soon taught her that off-track secret places or ditches were the best places to perform her natural functions. Now, luckily, she regards all pavements, roads, lawns and flower-beds as on-track and discreetly slopes off behind a rhododendron thicket or under some dense fir trees.

'Good with children.' Any children younger or less robust than my two would have been knocked flying by her energetic careering.

It took a year for her to stop looking hopeful at hearing distant voices, to understand that 'box' was not a punishment word and that if I popped out for half an hour, I would return. It was an awkward first year for her adjusting to new masters in a completely strange environment. Annoying for me was the oft repeated 'I told you so' and 'What did I say?' at every little setback: for example, stolen meat, shredded newspapers, puddles on the floor and refusals to emerge from the woods having learned their delights. It is galling that she has always loved him best.

Now that she is used to our little ways and eccentricities such as no dogs upstairs, no dogs on the real silk suite and our strange habit of sponging off the carefully applied cow pat or rolled-in horse manure, she is a paragon of virtue. And guess who takes the credit? Bimbo is so much a member of the family now that we cannot imagine life without her and after nine years we still congratulate ourselves constantly on our lucky choice. Bimbo seems happy enough with her lot too, if the ten-minute slathering greeting we are subjected to each new day is anything to go by. The Breadwinner has sometimes been known to miss his train on account of this mutual display and the ritual sharing of his tea and toast.

*   *   *

If, however, Bimbo could be said to have a fault it is jealousy. I would have to be very careful when dealing with those birds. Especially as Bimbo had been trained to hurl herself down to the kitchen garden barking furiously whenever I shouted, 'Birds!'

These two sparrows had acquired their names in the same such casual and haphazard way as the dog had. But what a mistake that turned out to be, as I was soon to find out. Oh that I had had the time to ponder on the merits of Icarus versus Pegasus (Peg for short)! Squeaker happens to be the unimaginative name of Bimbo's favourite plastic toy. When her strong white teeth clamp round it and she squeezes hard, it squeaks.

Back in the kitchen the birds were fed and tidied away under a feather duster, while I hastened to put on my poor-thing-toiling-over-a-hot-stove act.

I was babbling about the birds before the weary hunter had time to put his briefcase down.

'You're mad. Wasting your time. They'll never live. What's for dinner?' I was rather glad that it was not chicken.

'Do have a peep at them.'

It was a mistake to imagine that everyone would instantly fall in love with my foster babies as soon as they were seen. Harry was plainly dismayed by their immaturity. I think he had imagined little feathered things with bright beady eyes. If he was pessimistic about the survival of those figments, how much more was he so now that the minute and naked reality confronted him?

I thought to myself, if they stay alive until morning we have a chance. At 11 p.m. I gave them a last feed, changed the tissues covering the hamster bedding, covered the top of the flowerpot with the feather duster and put them into the airing cupboard.

5

The Muntjacs

At 6 a.m. I was up and onto the landing. Not a cheep to be heard. Out with the pot and off with the duster! They looked pink enough but still. Too still. Crouched like trussed oven-ready versions of Titania's Christmas dinner. Were they cold and dead or playing possum? My enquiring finger soon expelled all doubts. Up flew two wavering necks and screeching gapes. I rushed downstairs with them to stuff in chopped worms with soil, froghoppers and greenfly. Then I put the nest in a box over the pilot light of the cooker.

An hour seemed to be the longest interval they would suffer between meals so I was going to have to plan my expedition to the village ergonomically. It would save time if I did not collect my elderly mother and she puffed up the hill to my house so that we could leave straight after a feed. I hoped she hadn't much shopping to do.

My first port of call was the pet shop.

'Have you anything suitable for a newly hatched sparrow, please?'

'Well, what had you in mind?'

I had in mind large packets filled with fresh, small, easily digested nutritional foods. On the back of the packet it would declare: 'Only 10p. Ideal for newly hatched sparrows. Promotes *rapid growth* and *independence*. No artificial additives.' We peered without much hope into all the bins and sacks. Then I remembered the terrapins we used to keep. The ½oz. packet of dried tropical insects cost 75p. and I hoped they would be acceptable when reduced to powder and mixed with water.

The friendly manageress racked her brains at my insistent requests for the names of the customers who regularly bought bird seed from her. My humourless demands, brought about by having one eye on my watch and the other raking her shelves, brought to mind the Mafia demanding protection money. She finally capitulated:

'Well, there's one lady called Viv. I don't know her surname or telephone number, but I can tell you where she lives. She drives an ambulance and may be out now.'

I jumped into my car and soon found the house but no one was in. I would have to return in the evening.

Now for the library. With any luck there would be a carefully illustrated book entitled *How to Raise a SPARROW from Scratch. Recommended by the R.S.P.B.* Unfortunately there was nothing of the kind. As I had discovered from my own field guides at home the books available described the sparrow as an L.B.J. (little brown job) present throughout the British Isles. Food – grain, seeds and insects. The *Readers' Digest Birds of Britain* did, however, mention that the eggs hatch after eleven to fourteen days and the chicks can fly reasonably well in another two weeks or so. So, I had less than two weeks to think up a way of keeping from harm and feeding two small flying objects. Sufficient, however, unto the day thereof.

Back home within the hour poor Bimbo's joyous greeting was utterly ignored as I hastened to the oven. Not cooked but nice and warm and brought to instantaneous and vociferous boil with the raising of the lid (feather duster). I was pleased to note that the faeces were normal looking and what I would expect from nestlings. I don't know how I knew but I expect I had seen films of parent birds removing little white sacs from nests. Although it's not a thing I have consciously studied, as I am a keen gardener bird droppings are an everyday sight. I fed them on the last of the froghoppers and popped the feather duster back on top. This covering-up I had noticed produced an instantaneous effect. Silence.

I thought I would go through the woods to the warden's cottage. Chris Down and his family had a large assortment of creatures including birds. People often brought him injured birds and animals.

*　　　*　　　*

One snowy January Chris's wife Shirley had seen some tiny hoof tracks in the snow. She followed them to the public road and there saw a young Muntjac deer hopping around through the traffic. Shirley immediately dashed to the rescue. Catching it, she wrapped it in her anorak and returned through the swirling snow to the house. The vet came at once and pronounced it uninjured. Shirley acquired a baby bottle and fed it on watered-down cow's milk and some animal vitamins. The newcomer was a source of great interest to Val, the dog, who took it upon herself to be chief comforter and nurse. She used to lick it all over, paying particular attention to the rear end. This gentle massage encouraged the fawn to urinate which in turn made it eager for milk. The vet on his later visits was most impressed. Val had taught him something which no one had known about Muntjacs before.

After a few days Squeaker the Muntjac (yes, another imaginative naming) was put into a shelter rigged up in the garage as it was too hot for it in the house. It appeared to thrive but after ten days it died.

The Chinese Muntjac (*Muntjacus reevesi*) originate in Asia. Hertfordshire was one of the first places to be colonized by escapees from zoos or collections at the beginning of this century. They look at first sight like a medium-sized brown dog. Their movements however soon dispel this idea. I have seen them leap fences with such delicate grace that it makes the finest show jumper look like a cross between a carthorse and an elephant. The bucks have unbranched antlers up to four inches long pointing towards the back of the head and an interesting protruding razor-sharp tooth on either side of the top jaw. This tooth moves backwards and forwards in its socket. Both sexes have a scent gland located in front of each eye. The short tail is white underneath and is held erect when the animal is excited or running off. Rather like a rabbit's scut – and it probably serves the same warning purpose.

Muntjacs are very secretive but our familiarity with their features was brought about by an unfortunate but unavoidable collision with the car. It was a fine mature buck and I could not help thinking that at least it died quickly and that had it been a doe there may have been a fawn to suffer a lingering death.

A fairly busy road runs through the centre of this wooded area and at night there seems to be much toing and froing of the deer. It is quite a common sight to see their eyes reflected bright green in the headlights of the car. It is said that one was once seen to jump over a fence into the road then leap onto the bonnet of a passing car and off again into the woods on the other side.

A real success story was the case of the Muntjac which had leapt a boundary fence and had become entangled in the barbed wire stranded across the top. Its struggles were fortunately seen by a passing cyclist who went straight off to the warden's cottage for help. But how long had the poor creature been hanging like a discarded suede coat which had been flung over the fence after an accident with a pot of scarlet paint? Luckily Chris was in and armed with wire cutters soon extricated the poor animal. It had stripped all the skin from the whole of its underside and was in a parlous way. The trusty vet was once more summoned and did his best.

Shirley became a great favourite as she was the one who produced the food. Chris was not so popular as he was the one who had to hold it for the regular injections. After a while the great wound swelled up and turned black. Horrors. Gangrene? But no, pushing up underneath the huge scab was an entirely new hide. As soon as it was fit the Muntjac was released. It was taken to a clearing where it ran off like a cork from a bubbly bottle but when it realized it was in familiar surroundings it calmed down and was last seen contentedly grazing.

Bamba, a Muntjac doe, is a permanent resident with the warden. Although perfectly fit and healthy she can never be released as she thinks she is a dog and comes running up with wagging tail to lick your hand and have her head stroked. This behaviour would be fatal in the wild. Of course she is a source of great interest to visitors and a delightful pet but she must always be kept in the pen for her own safety. A woman in Buckingham-shire had picked her up as a fawn when her dogs had frightened the mother away. She took it home in the belief that the parent would not return. Actually this is not usually the case. When fawns, leverets and fairly mature fledglings are found, it is always best to leave them for their parents to find when you are out of the way. Unless, of course, you know the parents are dead.

However, Bamba finished up with our wood warden and Val the dog became her chief companion.

This by-product (unintentional taming) as a result of first aid or fostering was a problem that I would have to sort out should Squeaker and E.T. survive. And their survival was my immedi-ate problem now. Chris told me that when he fed his chickens on Layers' mash the posse of waiting sparrows zoomed in before he had time to tip it out. He generously gave me a small bag full and as it consisted mainly of ground-up mixed cereals I thought it would be ideal when mixed up with milk. On the way home I filled the plastic box with froghoppers.

Yveline arrived with a container of gentles and some very useful looking hairclips like long flat beaks which opened and shut by squeezing the ends. I have to admit that I do not like gentles, those legless white maggots, the larva of the bluebottle or blowfly. When I have seen them by the side of a fisherman on the riverbank I rapidly lose interest in his catch and hasten by with averted eyes, retching mildly.

I had prepared a chopping block and had a sharp knife ready.

'Look here, Yveline, I don't think I can tackle these just yet, will you do the honours?"

'But of course!'

I couldn't help peeping over my shoulder as I mixed a pinch

23

or two of Layers' mash in an egg cup. As soon as about six gentles were put onto the board they wriggled as fast as greased lightning to the edges of the board to escape. But there was no escaping the sharp knife wielded by Yveline's efficient hand. She looked as if it was something that she did every day of her life. However, I happen to know that she is terrified of spiders, which I rather like. Chacun à son goût.

'I have no feelings for these things. The birds are more important,' she said.

We each took a bird in one hand and a tweezer-like hairclip in the other. It took some unfortunate practice to manipulate them efficiently. On that first occasion, more often than not, the oozing half maggot was still clasped in the tweezers as I withdrew them from the gape. I was afraid of opening them too wide whilst they were lost from sight down the throat. The unsatisfied bird shrieked in frustration and it did not take long before panic forced me to employ a fingernail as well.

Suddenly Yveline noticed a little whitish lump like a blister the size of a petit pois on E.T.'s neck. Oh no, was it some injury we had not spotted? Was it pus? I examined Squeaker. A similar lump! But this one was Layers' mash coloured as well. Of course!

'It's their crops. How sweet.' Huge relief.

'Well in that case I think this one has had enough,' said Yveline firmly.' It looks as if it might burst.'

Now that we had discovered this rather elementary anatomical feature it proved to be a very good guide for feeding purposes. Sometimes they seemed to want food in less than one hour.

That second day they polished off gentles, dried tropical flies, Layers' mash, froghoppers, worms and water. I gave the last feed at nine o'clock and tumbled exhausted into bed. Had I or had I not seen a pin-point of shiny black in the centre of one of Squeaker's eye bulges just before I consigned them to the airing cupboard?

6

The Dingly-Danglies

Seven a.m. on day three and still alive! I was beginning to feel more confident. They had grown in the night. They took up more room in my hand and were more active. As I stuffed chopped worms, sieved hard-boiled egg and soaked and mashed dog biscuit down their throats, I spotted three tiny black pinholes gleaming from three covered eyeballs. Two belonging to Squeaker and one to E.T.

How strange they looked now. Dark grey five o'clock shadows on top of their skulls and down the backbones. Little fleshy stubs that were their tails. Could they see? Was I being watched? What did they think of their home (my kitchen)? They had never seen their parents nor their original nest so they must feel that these were normal surroundings for sparrows.

As soon as it became warmer today I must take them outside to hear sparrows and see if they responded. They must not become like Bamba the Muntjac and not recognize their own kind. I also wanted their own kind to recognize them. I had not given up hope that when they were fledged and flying the parents would respond to their begging and feed them.

I had noticed a rather large juvenile sparrow on the lawn being fed by what I termed the 'Gang of Four'. Mum, Dad, Aunt and Uncle. The youngster seemed to be quite capable of pecking up food for itself and it could certainly fly very well. With any luck the gang would take over mine, because how could I feed them when they were flying and too big for staying in a flowerpot? I had heard tales of parent birds with beaks full of food en route for their own nestlings being sidetracked by a larger gape and shriller begger. Sometimes even belonging to a different species.

This Thursday was another fine warm day and after the 10 a.m. feed I took them in my hand out onto the terrace. A male sparrow (Dad? Uncle?) was chirping loudly in a nearby rhododendron bush and to my delight both nestlings turned their heads to the noise. I felt like the mother whose baby first responds to the rattle. Not deaf, then! I would love to know if those tiny black dots could focus. I was looking forward to showing Yveline their latest development.

They did not want to sleep so much today and were climbing out of the flowerpot. I hastily substituted a 7″ flowerpot and pushed the bedding well down. In gardening circles it is known as 'potting on'. They were cheeping most of the time now. So noisy. So lusty. Pleased as I was with the progress I still felt I needed some expert advice. This evening I would seek out Viv, the bird-seed buyer.

Meanwhile the relentless search for food must go ahead. A pair of tights with the feet cut off and the legs knotted with the waist stretched and sewn round a pulled-open wire coat hanger made a fairly good moth and insect net. With a 'Walkies!', it was off to the woods once more. Bimbo was slightly puzzled with this new game: the Mistress shaking ferns and dancing on the spot to the accompaniment of her own new private swear word, *'Passer domesticus!'* interspersed with 'I'll get you, you little blighter!'

My dainty arabesques and allemandes soon degenerated into frustrated lunges and gallops. Bimbo began to bark, drawing unwanted attention to this middle-aged party who was puce, panting and perspiring as the pretty little white moths spiralled and zig-zagged out of reach.

It was obvious that I was not their only predator and years of evading capture had made them evolve this very effective dodging dance. My high hopes of the tights bulging with moths, caterpillars and other goodies soon faded and when I counted the miserable catch I decided that all that effort was not worth four moths, one of which escaped as I was counting them. Besides, I did not mind being observed collecting froghoppers – I was becoming a familiar sight with my plastic box – as I could be mistaken for a scientist on serious research, but my cavorting with the tights could be misunderstood.

Normally in June it is impossible to walk in these woods without coming back draped with a bead curtain of what we locals call 'dingly-danglies'. Some have such evocative names for such disagreeable caterpillars and insignificant moths. Amongst them are 'waves', 'seraphims', 'carpets', 'pugs' and 'emeralds'. The real culprits here, however, are the 'oak roller' (*Tortrix viridana*) which can entirely strip a tree of leaves, the 'buff tip' (*Phalera bucephala*), the 'mottled umber' (*Erannis defoliaria*) and the 'winter moth' (*Operophtera brumata*). For the last two years these woods, about five hundred acres in extent, have been stripped of their young foliage in spring. The oak, birch, hawthorn, blackthorn, hazel and aspen have looked like winter trees in June. When I stood still I swear I could hear the chomping of millions of jaws. It was more probably the rustling of the falling chewed-off pieces of leaves which sometimes made quite a thick carpet underfoot. Like a strange green autumn. Later in the year they put forth new leaves and I wondered how long the trees would survive this treatment year after year. I remember it was lovely for the birds and birdwatchers alike. The denuded canopy revealed the willow warblers, chiffchaffs, wood warblers and friends having a bonanza.

This year it was quite different. Nature has a way of balancing things out and the glossy fresh foliage with not so much as a nibble out of it seemed to mock me in my desperate search.

7

The Bird-Seed Buyer and
the Art Show

That evening I stood on a stranger's doorstep. 'Viv? I'm sorry I don't know your other name so I couldn't phone first but I wonder if you can help me? It's about these birds . . .'

As soon as it was apparent that I was neither an encyclopaedia saleswoman nor a double-glazing agent, I was invited in and proper introductions were made. It turned out that I had been to the local infant school with Vivienne's husband Ron.

Vivienne listened to my story quite taking it for granted that I should be so worried and desperate about the lives of two sparrows. I know that one pair of sparrows only needs to rear two babies to maturity during their whole lifetime to keep numbers of the species constant. If everybody interfered with nature like me we would soon be knee deep. I do know that.

I suppose most people are familiar with the case of the European Sparrow in America. About a dozen times from 1850 onwards the sparrow was deliberately introduced into the United States; about 1,800 were imported in twenty years. The hope was that they would check the ravages of the destructive elm-tree caterpillar and they no doubt did some good that way. But they found themselves in conditions of material well-being and multiplied exceedingly. They found abundant food, convenient nesting places, unlimited room and no enemies. In a few years they inundated the continent, pushing out or just tolerating native birds and feeding voraciously on corn.

Well, two sparrows would not upset the balance of nature greatly. Vivienne said that she had tried to raise sparrows without success. One was brought to her rather badly damaged and finally it had to be put to sleep. Another lived for two weeks. It had acquired its feathers and was flying but just when Vivienne thought she had succeeded, for no apparent reason it died. I was warned not to be too hopeful as sparrows were difficult to rear.

Vivienne actually takes newly hatched parakeets and hand rears them on baby food. Strawberry yoghurt is a great favourite. This hand rearing has a twofold advantage for a breeder. It makes the mother lay another egg and her offspring becomes very tame.

Once when a hen budgerigar died, Vivienne took the two eggs and hatched them in her bra. One of the chicks died but the other was kept in a container in the same cosy place. As it grew and became noisier, many were the strange glances cast in her direction. In a local supermarket one day she sought to allay the worries of puzzled customers by casually remarking that there wasn't a bird trapped in the freezer, but that the funny noise was a budgie in her bra. It did not seem to allay their fears at all!

I learned that over the years people have often brought the rescued victims of cats or cars to this capable person. In fact one of the local vets has her telephone number on hand to give to worried bird owners. This came home to roost neatly when Vivienne once telephoned for help about a sickly parakeet and was given her own number to ring for advice.

Often the birds brought are too injured and shocked to be helped, but the story of Goldie the mistle thrush reminds me of Bamba the Muntjac. Goldie first arrived as a miserable, broken, unidentifiable scrap. With care and digestive biscuits, hard-boiled egg yolk and so on he lived with the budgerigars for seven years, when he died of old age quite happy in the belief that he was a big budgerigar. At night the birds all went to sleep on a long perch wing to wing. The otherwise symmetrical row of little coloured humps was interrupted by a large dark hump.

A cat-mauled blue tit which was never able to fly also lived in Vivienne's care until it also died of old age.

Once a robin which was being treated for injury was put in the outside aviary and every day the local robin came to court her. Finally the patient was well enough to be released and although they did not exactly fly off into the sunset together, they did stay as a pair in the vicinity which was a highly satisfactory end to the story.

Regarding my sparrows, Vivienne suggested that I did not give them so much water and that I must keep them really warm and not forget that the airing cupboard gets cold in the wee small hours when the heater is off. She wished me luck and I returned home with mixed feelings.

I thought I had got the food right. Probably more balanced than that proffered by the average hopeful rearer. But until Squeaker and E.T. were past the crucial two weeks I was not going to be complacent. I had better start dismantling the eye-level grill on the cooker so that the box containing the flowerpot could rest over the pilot light on the oven all night.

Day four and at 7.30 a.m. two slightly sleepy nestlings managed to swallow soaked Layers' mash, moths and chopped earthworms. By now there often appeared on the doorstep little contributions from friends and acquaintances of moths in jam jars and worms in yoghurt pots.

By 9 a.m. they were ravenous and downed soaked dried insects, egg and Layers' mash. In the seven subsequent meals that day they managed to put away froghoppers, moths, egg, gentles, cereal, dried insects, worms, Layers' mash, insects and soaked dog biscuit. With all that fuel they were becoming very active and their wings seemed to have grown. Their crops were no longer petit pois size but more like ordinary peas.

Yveline came round at lunchtime to assist with feeding. I always seemed to pick out Squeaker first and I thought: I'm being partial. I must treat them the same, no favouritism.

'Yveline, you choose. Which one would you like?'

'I don't mind. You choose. Why don't you have Squeaker?' No help there.

'Oh, all right.'

Apart from trying to be fair we should change from time to time to get them both used to being handled by another, I thought. Besides, dear little E.T. was smaller and needed more care.

But it was curious that however logically I lectured myself, I did have a favourite. Was I like that with my own children? I don't think so. I used to have a dream when they were young that we were all in the sea and they were drowning. I was only allowed to save one and they were both equally within reach. Which one would I choose? I never ever made the decision even in my innermost secret thoughts. Fortunately they both learned to swim at an early age and that was the end of that particular nightmare.

The following day was Saturday and Harry and I were due to attend a luncheon party and official opening of an art exhibition. Yes, Yveline would gladly have them. It would be no trouble to keep them locked away from Sooty the English Setter, Goldie the Spaniel and Minou the Persian cat.

Saturday dawned bright and sunny again and at 7 a.m. the birds were vigorous and lively. The night over the pilot light seemed to suit them. At the 9.30 a.m. feed they were even more vigorous and lively and they began to fight with each other. Wouldn't you know it. Just like their human counterparts; as soon as you want them to be on their best behaviour and no trouble to the babysitter, they start playing up.

Later Harry and I were nibbling celery sticks and cheese sandwiched between large crusty hunks of 'culture'.

'Well what do you think of A's expressionless environmental style?'

'Now don't you think B's still lives are even livelier this year?'

'Oh, positively leaping.'

'I say, how about old C then? Abstractions of the abstract. Doesn't know, poor thing, that that's a real no no now.'

'I love this super super-realism, don't you?'

'Oh, yes, yes, but the *main* thing is . . .' and here I paused while expectant and interested faces waited for my profound and considered analysis of the current trend. With this cross-section of literate and knowledgeable people there surely must be one . . ?

' . . . The *main* thing is, does anyone know anything about baby birds?' . . . Ah, symbolism!

'Well no, actually. I know! Why don't you have some more wine?'

Meanwhile, back at the ranch, according to the diary notes of the babysitter, Squeaker and E.T. were enjoying chopped worms, froghoppers, soaked dog biscuits, gentles, tropical insects with Layers' mash, more worms and froghoppers. Salut!

My little charges greeted my return clamorously. Their feathers had actually appeared during my absence and their tails were now ¾" long. After a last feed at 10 p.m., I put the pot in a large wastepaper basket over the pilot light.

8

E.T.'s Narrow Escape

The next day they were standing up in the nest and happy to be picked out. This was also the day that Harry and I were going to Sunday lunch at Henry and Yveline's to meet their friends and their small daughter. The birds would come too, of course.

Henry, Yveline's husband, noticed how they had grown. Yveline and I were like proud parents. Our similarly named spouses watched indulgently as we enthused:

'Look at the feathers down their backs!'

'See their *real* wings!'

'Aren't they pretty?'

'Now it's one o'clock, we must remember to feed them at two sharp.' How could I forget? I had taken to wearing a pendant watch pinned with a large safety pin to my chest. It ruled my life.

We shut them safely away from the two dogs, one cat and small child. At due intervals Yveline and I departed the company and shut ourselves in to feed and coo over our little nestlings. Not for the first time it occurred to me that whilst the birds were like babies in carry-cots and portable, my social life would not suffer. Soon – and very soon too, if their rate of growth continued at this pace – they would become the equivalent of over-active toddlers. Social pariahs.

The following day they were getting so strong that I had difficulty holding them both in one hand as I used the other to proffer food. They snatched at anything in sight, including each other's heads. Then one, more nimble, leapt out of my hand and bolted up the sleeve of my right arm. They still had a distinct preference for darkness and loved being under the feather duster or inside the front of my cardigan as I sat indoors in the evening.

It was E.T. who had dashed for cover up my sleeve and was now scrabbling with tiny needle-sharp claws for purchase on my skin. I popped the squeaking Squeaker back into the nest and tried to shake E.T. down my arm into my waiting cupped hand. This merely frightened the bird and it scrambled up as high as the elbow so I could now no longer bend my arm. I could not pull the garment off as there was no 'give' in the thick material and as soon as I pulled at the cuff I could feel E.T. being squashed against my elbow. The sleeve was straight and tight fitting and I did not see how the frightened bird would be able to breathe much longer.

Oh, what a silly way to die. I was on the floor by this time, having removed myself like Houdini out of the rest of the garment with the idea of encouraging E.T. to climb further and out by way of armpit and neck hole. No more movement. Had it suffocated already? With my right arm held stiffly out in front, I found the scissors and with my left hand tried to cut the material. It was a forlorn hope as I cannot comb my hair or clean my teeth with my left hand, let alone manipulate scissors.

Don't panic. Think. But not for too long – it was ominously quiet and still in the sleeve. As far as I could tell there were three possible solutions.

The easiest would be to go into the front garden and call to a passer-by and ask them to cut the sleeve. Unfortunately, there did not seem to be any passers-by on foot (there very rarely are) and a half-dressed woman waving a pair of scissors would be unlikely to get a strange motorist to stop.

Well, who could I telephone to get here in time? Yveline was out and so were my other nearest neighbours. My mother did not hear the phone. I was wasting valuable breathing time, it would have to be the third solution. Kill or cure. I had tried running my left hand up the sleeve but it could not get far enough and had only served to panic the bird into a tighter position. Approaching from the shoulder end had encouraged it to sink its claws deeply into the felty material. The situation reminded me of a tale of a wartime hero who escaped from countless battles unscathed only to be run over by a bus as soon as he returned home. Well, E.T., I'll do my best to save you. Whispering soothing bedside nothings, I hung my arm straight down (both birds always seemed to want to climb upwards), then relaxed my muscles in that arm until it was as thin and soft as possible. Then with real and sincere apologies and deter-mined and sustained tugs at the cuff, dragged the sleeve down my arm. I hoped E.T.'s bones were like those of a hamster or were young enough to be bendy. There was an outraged shrieking, then the sleeve was off. I extricated the clinging claws and returned the scarlet and hysterical nestling to its sibling in the flowerpot.

The rest of the seventh day passed without further drama. Their eyes were opening nicely so I took them out into the garden several times to hear and see the other sparrows. I had previously tried putting them in the centre of the lawn sur-

34

rounded by crumbs to encourage their parents down to feed them, but the baby sparrows were totally ignored in favour of the white bread. That experiment soon had to come to an end in any event, as it did not take long for the collared doves and wood pigeons to swoop down, followed by rather more sinister visitors in the form of jays, crows and magpies.

9

Travelling Birds

Tuesday. The day for handing in my list of produce for the flower show to be held in our local village hall this coming Saturday. The garden, as far as I could tell after repeated scourings, was absolutely devoid of damaging insect life. Every curled or distorted leaf had been examined for potential protein, which, if in residence, had been plucked out and put in the plastic box. I had, ironically, that very day, found a single cabbage white butterfly, the first I had seen that season. I carefully caught it and eased it under the protective netting on the cabbage patch. Go to it, butterfly! How long would it take the eggs to hatch into peck-sized food, I wondered. Every lettuce that I took to the kitchen was washed most carefully and the water poured through a fine-meshed sieve. Sometimes there was nothing to show for my effort. I had never known a year like it.

My constant treks to the woods had now completely cleared the froghoppers from the first four hundred yards of greenery abutting the track. Open tracks and edges of clearings seemed to be my best hunting grounds.

I had had the birds exactly a week and how different they looked now. Today they were looking like real miniature sparrows. The feathers and beaks were developing well and they began to flutter and test their wings. When Yveline came in the afternoon we took them onto the lawn. They tried to fly but were too wobbly on the ground and scuttled back to our hands and the comforting darkness under our clothes. Yveline's shoulder-length thick hair was a great attraction.

I thought, if they are trying to fly, they must learn to perch properly. I took a strong cardboard grocery box large enough for them to exercise in and inserted a garden cane through both sides so that it made a perch about one inch from the base. I put their nest and feather duster in the corner of the box and a wire grid covered with a cloth over the top. This became a convenient new home for them whilst they were in the house.

Today I introduced crushed walnut and tinned dog food into their diet. The tray of food, serving implements, tissues, cotton wool, small containers, sharp knife and chopping board occupied the Windsor chair in the kitchen. Much to the chagrin of Bimbo whose favourite look-out post it was. A well known firm of chocolate makers sold their product in a most useful sturdy transparent box with a hinged lid – ideal for the egg cups of more perishable food like scrambled egg which had to be kept in the refrigerator. Also in the refrigerator were the round tubs of living gentles. The cold stopped their growth and prevented them pupating, but as soon as they were taken out and put onto the chopping block they sprang into wriggling but sharply curtailed life.

Poor Bimbo could not understand all the frenzied activities and strange smells. And why was she shouted at and reproved whenever she wanted to try out those new squeaking toys? I always tried to make a fuss of her at the same time as I was dealing with the birds but it was difficult without a third hand. I was reminded of the time of Gemma's birth which took place at home in order to minimize sibling jealousy. The very first morning when I was in bed feeding and drooling over my new baby, I heard a toddler's footsteps on the stairs so I snatched the newborn infant from my breast and thrust her to the end of the bed just in time to greet elder sister with both arms free and open wide for the usual morning cuddle.

Bimbo finally solved her jealousy problem by utterly ignoring the birds and refusing to remain in their presence. One evening as I sat on the sofa with Bimbo curled under my hand at my side, a bird in my cardigan woke up and gave a soft tweet. Bimbo jumped back in outrage as if my hand had turned into a viper. Her look of betrayed trust smote me and despite my pleadings she slid off the sofa and made for the door, disgust in every stiff movement.

On the Wednesday I was going to a small luncheon followed by a further visit to the art exhibition. As Yveline was not available to babysit the birds would have to go too. How would my hostess take to a box of birds in her spare room and a strange box of food in her fridge? Better not take gentles and worms. Egg and soaked dog biscuit and just a few froghoppers in a plain wrapping.

I gave the birds a hearty feed and changed all the soiled tissues. Then I carefully eased them in their new box onto the back seat of my Mini for the fifteen-mile drive to Radlett. Unlike Toad, they did not care for motoring. Tweets of fright interspersed with shrieks of displeasure were only somewhat minimized by hearing my voice. I kept up a loud, reassuring chatter: 'Never mind the nasty noise, my pets. Soon be there, my darlings and you shall have eggy to eat. Hush, my pretty ones, Mother is here . . .' I expect passing motorists thought I was singing to myself. I had one or two odd looks but that was probably because I was creeping along at twenty-five miles an hour, even on the dual carriageway.

Once arrived, the birds were on their best behaviour and feeding was accomplished with the minimum of disruption. They also happily wolfed down some rice left over from our meal.

Back home I served the Breadwinner with steak and the birds with gentles, tinned sweetcorn and dog food. They were fluttering and trying to perch. After their last feed at 10.30 p.m. I was beginning to feel more confident about their survival.

*   *   *

Day ten. Squeaker and E.T. were feeding voraciously and were very lively. I had to keep checking myself from being rather smug. It was early days yet and that strange failure after fourteen days that Vivienne had mentioned and that I had heard from other people preyed on my mind. 'Other people' included the gas fitter, the milkman, any callers to the house including those known to members of the household and complete strangers. I felt I should leave no stone unturned in my search for knowledge gained from the experience of others.

The Jehovah's Witnesses, deliverymen and gas fitters were all sooner or later interrupted in their monologues on God in Society Today, and variations on the theme of the age of my gas boiler, its calibration and thermostatic control, with a firm 'Yes, but do you happen by any chance to have raised a baby bird?' I always seemed to get the same response, 'What sort?'

I felt like saying the sort mentioned in the Bible as dropping to the ground and God knowing all about it. But I could not remember the exact quotation and invariably found myself apologizing for them not being robins, bald-necked eagles nor even pretty thrushes.

'Well, er, well, they are actually just sparrows.'

It was an eye-opener how the most unexpected folk came up with snippets of information and concern and how those I would have expected to be interested – naturalists, country lovers and some children – did not. I was quite touched by a New Zealand visitor to a neighbour's house using some of her precious short time in this country to catch moths for me. Another couple frequently made a one-mile trip to deposit offerings of worms and also introduced chopped currants for the fledglings' delectation. I of course understand lack of interest – I'm not wild about train spotting or computer games – but laughter and revulsion took me by surprise.

This day the birds were trying to fly but were not very good at

perching. As it was warm I took them out several times to hear
their parents and practice flying. They still ran to me for cover
though. Once I left them in the centre of the lawn and watched
from behind the magnolia tree as a female sparrow came down
and led them to the shrubbery. As soon as they were hidden she
flew off and made no attempt to feed them. I was glad to see an
adult take an interest and seemingly recognize them as two of
her own kind despite their close contact with humans.

Another visit to the lawn in the afternoon interested an adult
male sparrow but he soon flew off. A blackbird came down for a
look too. The young ones were ravenous; all that exercise, I
expect.

That evening, under my jumper, one of them began preening
for the first time. Their last meal of the day was at 11.15 p.m. and
consisted of froghoppers and Layers' mash with egg. It had
been such a happy evening as I could now see that they were
capable of developing typical bird activities, preening, pecking,
flying and so forth, without parents or other birds to show
them. I felt for the first time less anxious for their future.

As a consequence the blow that befell the next day was all the
more horrible.

10

Pangs of Guilt and an
Interesting Discovery

I was not particularly worried when I went downstairs at 7.30
the next morning and all was quiet in the box. After all, they had
had a late night. I pottered round the kitchen preparing food for
the humans in the house and when the noise of my activity
failed to elicit a squeak, I had a sudden frightened thought. I
snatched the covering off the box and Squeaker squeaked. Oh,
thank the gods. But E.T. was lying in a corner with glazed eyes.

It was alive and trying to stand and squeak but could not.

I picked it up and made a warm nest of my hand and offered water which was swallowed. I tried offering all sorts of food but it was refused and as I was distressing the bird I did not persist. What had gone wrong? What had I given them to eat yesterday? Checking the notebook I saw that their food had been just as usual, nothing new introduced. I was beginning to suffer pangs of guilt. Had I always made sure that the gentler E.T. had had its fair share at meal times? Was this punishment for partiality?

How was Squeaker? It was difficult to tell but he seemed more subdued and refused the chopped worms. Maybe that was because he was growing up and needed more grain type foods. He took some gentles, however. Then I noticed that the droppings were rather watery.

I telephoned Yveline and broke the news but she was cheerful as usual.

'Don't worry. E.T. will be all right.'

I made E.T. as comfortable as possible in a soft nest under the feather duster and resolved not to make what I was convinced were its last hours miserable by trying to feed it when it manifestly did not like being disturbed.

At ten o'clock I took Squeaker to the garden where he flew about quite strongly but not always finishing where he was aiming. On one amateurish zoom about four feet from the ground Squeaker was obviously aiming for the rhododendrons and firs near the boundary. Suddenly with a swoosh of wings a male bird dived underneath Squeaker, rose up until he was supporting him on his back and flapped his wings rapidly underneath until they were both high in a silver birch tree. The adult bird then flew off leaving Squeaker firmly perched well out of my reach. And there he stayed. I called, cajoled and offered bribes. Squeaker replied but did not budge.

This is what I had been dreading. Had I been a sparrow I could have flown up and fed him but my efforts with the ladder had only succeeded in frightening him to an even more inaccessible perch. At least he did not seem to want to fly any more so I could go indoors from time to time to inspect E.T. Poor E.T. was definitely moribund and even Yveline had to admit to it when she came to see in the afternoon.

Finally at two o'clock Squeaker's hunger overcame his fright (surely not vertigo?) and he came down to my hand and ate just two gentles. Then he flew off to the rhododendron thicket. Later he flew to a tall conifer on the boundary of my garden. This time an adult female materialized out of an empty sky and fluttered underneath lifting him to a firm perch. She also left at once.

Suddenly the penny dropped! Why had Gemma said on that first day, '. . . a lot of squeaking. Actually, I thought I saw an *adult fluttering* down.' Of course she did. A parent was supporting its precociously flying – actually falling – youngster. That was why they were not injured. That was why they finished up on the terrace, not directly under the nest. They had been carried.

The garden next door harboured neither cats nor dogs and the next garden, about one hundred odd feet further on, was Yveline's.

Squeaker called continuously so I knew where he was and could just see that he was running his beak along tiny twigs. Learning to find his own food; but what on earth could be found on a few dry conifer twigs? I offered scrambled egg and all the other favourites but to no avail.

Yveline and I went next door and called and called and finally at half-past ten when it was quite dark Squeaker no longer answered. Back at the house I found that E.T. was now quite dead.

11

The Bumble Bee Nest

After a mainly sleepless night, I dragged myself out to the garden to call and look for Squeaker. Each time I called, 'Squeaker!' Bimbo dashed round and round in huge circles (just out of reach), clenching her teeth on her plastic toy which emitted the most tiresome and nerve-jangling squeals and squeaks.

In the normal way I would have played with the dog, pleased that she knew the name of her toy, encouraging her to pounce on it when I threw it and engage in growling tug-of-wars in pretend ownership disputes. But now it was different. An irritation hardly to be borne. As I lunged for the bright plastic object I could see that she thought at least she had incited co-operation, and she pranced teasingly beyond my reach, squeezing and squeaking the toy madly. How could I hear if the living Squeaker was calling?

'O.K. That's enough. Clear off. Take the flaming thing away.' Her puzzlement was plain and she resorted to hysterical barking and even more frenzied activities. It was becoming like a living nightmare. And this was the morning of the year when I would usually be calmly and smugly trotting around with trowel, scissors and trug, gathering and arranging my entries for the flower show.

I trailed down through the lower lawns and through the espaliers to the kitchen garden. My lips were becoming quite sore with being constantly pursed to make the squeaking kissing noise that I had trained the birds to open their beaks to. This morning my trowel was going to be used for a much sadder activity. E.T.'s grave. Better get it over with now.

On my way back to the house I suddenly saw a very small juvenile sparrow hopping towards me! I stepped eagerly for-

42

ward, hands outstretched. But it flew off and I sagged back into despondency as I realized that it was the one I had seen with the gang which fed it from time to time.

I could hear Bimbo howling which meant the telephone was ringing. Henry's voice:

'Bring food. Yveline's got Squeaker.'

I raced along the street with unbrushed teeth and bare feet. I tried to stay calm as all three of us gulped back tears of joy. The Squeaker was clinging tightly to Yveline's shoulder underneath her hair and he looked as if he was never going to budge again.

As we sat on the terrace sipping tea and proffering tempting chopped worms towards Yveline's neck, I heard how she had called from her bedroom window and then from the breakfast table on the terrace. After a lonely night in the trees Squeaker now seemed to realize on which side his toast was buttered and he had homed in to the familiar voice like a pigeon to its loft.

But I could not let him stay here; it was not safe with the dogs and cat. So I hastened back to my house clutching my foolish little bird to my bosom.

'I was so *worried*. Now *promise* you won't do that again. You silly little bird (kiss, kiss). You're too young to be out at night. The chilly dew will get you.'

Perhaps I ought to cage him temporarily? At least until he could feed himself? But how would he learn to be a normal bird and feed himself in a cage? Besides, the idea just repulsed me. There are too many prisoners in this world. I wanted Squeaker to be independent, wild and free. Not too wild. I wanted to be able to keep track of him, to know all this effort was not in vain.

On this sunny day, however, he seemed quite content to sit around in low trees and shrubs, occasionally calling for attention or answering my calls. Sometimes I called him onto my shoulder to be fed, other times I handed food to him on his perch.

The great tits had not reared their young in their box this year so I thought I'd empty it out to see why they had deserted. As I

43

opened the box an angry high-pitched buzzing erupted. Treasure trove! A bumble bee nest about the size of an orange. I noticed the deserted eggs of the great tit underneath. There was a furious buzzing as I tipped it onto the lawn and tore apart the soft leathery covering of the cells to scoop out the fat white larvae curled one to each open hexagonal cell. What a feast for my Squeaker! Won't he be glad he came home. It was a bit of a battle and I decided to leave the contents of the capped cells as my conscience was beginning to smite me as were the brave little workers who were so noisily protecting their home. I bundled the lot up making sure that the queen was inside and thrust it all back into the nesting box. Then I closed it and remounted it onto the tree. I hoped they would be able to repair the damage my too eager fingers had wrought. I had deliberately left the eggs and the pupae. I'm sorry, bumble bees.

'Come Squeaker, treatettes!'

Squeaker, having re-fuelled with the succulent goodies, essayed a flight to the rhododendrons. Halfway across the lawn he was joined by the juvenile sparrow who closely flapped underneath until both were perched side by side on a rhododendron branch. The juvenile turned to Squeaker, crouched down, spread and quivered its wings and opened its beak wide in the traditional 'begging' posture. Squeaker followed suit. The first time I had ever seen him do it. Oh, why couldn't he have done it to an adult? The gang were still around. His parents even now passing the time by copulating noisily on the roof.

After clashing open beaks fruitlessly the juvenile hopped back a step and had a think. Then to my astonishment he/she mounted Squeaker, presuming the still crouching Squeaker to be in the female receptive pose. I suppose it was trying to copy Dad on the roof. They both fell off the branch and I decided it was time to intervene. Enough confusion was enough. Squeaker was quite pleased to hop onto my hand and be put into the magnolia tree nearer the back door.

Whilst they are young male and female sparrows look alike

44

with plumage similar to that of a female sparrow: pale brown with the darker brown wing and tail feathers edged with pale brown and a pale buff stripe over each eye. Neither Squeaker nor his young friend had yet acquired the eye stripe. I was just guessing that Squeaker was male, but I had no thoughts about E.T. either way. It would be winter before I knew for sure.

Although Squeaker had fed well all day his droppings were watery and at half past eight that evening I made a nest and perch in a basket in the utility room.

Loud chirruping from my little brown bird perched on the handle of the basket greeted the dawn of Sunday July 8th. Day thirteen. It was to be the hottest day we had had this year. Squeaker spent a great deal of time sheltering on a perch under the roof of the bird table. He did not seem to want to explore so much today. I was just as pleased as I was expecting my brother and sister-in-law for strawberries, raspberries and homemade sparkling wine in the afternoon.

At lunchtime Squeaker came to find me instead of just calling and I fed him on ant's eggs which I dug from under the decorative York stone. He fed every hour and after a supper of shortcake crumbs left over from our feast he went to sleep in the basket in the utility room. Things seemed to be working out more easily than I had hoped.

12

To the Vet

Monday morning early I cheerfully trotted downstairs to the utility room looking forward to seeing my miniature feathered friend perched cutely on the basket handle.

Strange. No happy calling of recognition. No bird.

My heart lurched. I snatched up the feather duster and there was Squeaker. No longer squeaking. Just opening his beak with no sound coming out. What had happened to his voice? Why wasn't he hopping around? The symptoms were ominously like those of E.T. but I managed to feed him on froghoppers and caterpillars.

By nine o'clock he was still quite silent and crouched under the feather duster. His eyes were half closed and glazed.

My hands were trembling as I frantically searched the directories for vets' telephone numbers. I tried the nearest first but there was no reply. Finally I managed to contact the receptionist of a veterinary practice in Hatfield, seven miles away.

'I'm on my way with a dying sparrow. Can you please find out if there are any bird specialists I can contact?'

A quick check on Squeaker confirmed that the open shallow basket and feather duster would be a suitable means of transport. This bird would not be flying out and off anywhere today. I burst into silly tears as I fumblingly prepared soft foods for the journey.

As I raced my bumping Mini along the roads there were no alarmed shrieks of displeasure nor even quiet tweets of protest from the basket on the seat beside me.

Rounding a rather dangerous corner at a somewhat faster speed than usual, I startled a flock of sparrows up from the road.

'Out of the way you stupid birds or I'll mow you all down.' I blared on the horn but hardly braked.

Now wait a minute! This does not make sense. Get a grip of yourself. Have a sense of proportion. First, stop blubbering; the vet will listen with more attention if you are calm and collected. Secondly, a sparrow is a sparrow and those birds on the road have as much right to life as Squeaker. Thirdly, it is a longish journey so drive more carefully. And while you are at it, work out why those starving and dying *human beings* you saw on television did not galvanize you into immediate fund-raising activities? And why are you still crying, you fool?

There were three other patients waiting with their blank-faced owners. A noisy black dog – nothing much wrong with him, anyone could see that. A cat in a basket clutched by an elderly lady and a young lady nursing a covered bird cage. I sat down beside her. She might know something about birds.

I'm one of those irritating people who feel it is their bounden social duty to break those awful tense silences one finds in train carriages, surgeries or at parties, with stimulating remarks to encourage meaningful interaction and conversation.

'What's wrong with pussy, then?' Brightly and too loudly. I saw the feather duster stir as Squeaker responded to the sound of my voice. Every time I interposed a 'Poor thing' or 'Fancy that' into the low monologue to which the elderly lady was treating me, the duster heaved and I heard little distressed scrabblings.

It seemed like seven and a half hours before pussy was beckoned into the surgery, and I turned in relief to the young woman with the bird cage. My real objective all along. I must disguise my voice though, it was upsetting Squeaker.

'What have you got there, then?' I hissed out of the side of my mouth.

'Me budgie.'

'O dear, what's wrong with it?' Perhaps it had the same symptoms as Squeaker and it was a commonplace thing, easily curable.

'It's in to 'ave its toenails clipped.'

Lord save me, had I to wait for that performance to be over before my turn?

'I have a very sick bird, a sparrow, under this feather duster.' There was a long silence. Was she considering secession? Was the dying bird to be given precedence over the budgie's pedicure? No such luck. Talon trimming had priority.

'Don't you feel embarrassed walking around with that?' And she sniggered in embarrassment for me.

It certainly had the effect of shutting me up for a while as in astonishment I pondered on the vanity of humans. But I could not let it go.

47

'It would never occur to me to be embarrassed at anything I was doing if it was the right thing in the circumstances. If my sick bird felt more at ease in a potty on my head, I'd walk down the High Street like that too.'

It was a relief to us both when the budgie was called in.

My turn next! The vet had a good bedside manner with owners. I think he could see from the wild look in my eye that I would not accept chloroform as a humane solution. I related the sad tale of E.T. who had had the self-same symptoms.

'Our bird expert is working for a zoo now. Crested cranes, parrots, you know. Now this little fellow sounds as if it has respiratory trouble.'

Thank the gods, a sort of diagnosis. My sparrow was being taken seriously.

'I'll give you some dog antibiotic. One drop per four pounds in weight.'

'Let's do it *now*.' I said. 'I'll open the beak and you put the appropriate amount on this scrambled egg.'

By now the receptionist had joined us; perhaps it was the mention of E.T. (the space alien) that had drawn her. Our three heads bent over Squeaker to calculate his almost negative weight. Our three heads drew back simultaneously as we tried some rapid mental arithmetic. The vet worked it out first:

'Well, just a sort of smidgen, don't you think?'

'Yes, yes, the merest smear.'

Squeaker jerked convulsively and the egg went down. It was a lucky shot as the beak opening and swallowing were slightly out of sequence now.

'Shall I keep trying to force feed him?' Thinking of E.T. It seemed blindingly obvious when the vet explained that the more food that went down the more strength the bird would have. Poor E.T.

Back in the car I managed to force a few chopped gentles down a weary but trying-to-be-helpful throat. The fine weather had broken and it started to rain as I drove home.

I reassembled a nest in a box over the pilot light of the oven and gently transferred a rather weak and floppy Squeaker. Then I stowed the precious antibiotic in the fridge and dashed off to the woods for a further supply of froghoppers.

The day passed in a miserable daze and the weather wept in sympathy. Feeding was becoming quite difficult and I was obviously upsetting Squeaker by waking him up to push food and water down his wavering gape. If I didn't he would surely die just like E.T. Fairly quickly and as nature had intended fourteen days ago.

The mother had already laid a fresh clutch of eggs, I suspected. There was already one healthy juvenile with the Gang of Four. They only needed to raise one between them each year for four years to have replaced themselves. There was no room in nature for weak and sickly specimens. Especially those with poor nest-building and defenestration characteristics. Even if my Squeaker were healthy physically, who knows what mental damage I had already caused. Did he really know he was a sparrow and would his natural instincts develop without early contact with adult birds? Would he know how to shelter and feed himself? His first foray into the big wide world, the neighbours' garden, had nearly ended in disaster. This bird had learned to come to me and look for me. When I called to find out where he was perched, he always replied. He called to me when he saw me emerge from the house. But now he was a voiceless, nestbound invalid.

Sparrows are normally so wary of humans. Not like the blackbird or daring robin who stays so close to the gardener that he is in danger of decapitation by the spade. No, sparrows have good reason to fear humans. Having decided to live in or near the dwellings of man in order to enjoy the fruits of man's labour in the way of corn and household scraps, they have had to put up with being caught for the pot in return.

In the sixteenth century sparrows were accepted as rent if

nothing better was available and several dozen were offered at a time. They were also caught to feed hawks. Young boys with bows and arrows were sent to the grain fields to kill them.

John Skelton (1460–1529) wrote 'The Sparrow's Dirge' which features a nunnery in Norfolk and its menu:

> For the soul of Philip Sparrow
> That was late slain at Carrow
> Among the Nunnes Black,
> For that sweet soules sake
> And for all sparrows' Souls
> Set in our bread-rolls,
> Pater noster qui
> With an Ave Mari.

I guiltily wondered what I was doing as all day I tortured that poor unfortunate creature and forced food and medicine into his body.

'You were right,' I said to my Breadwinner as he returned that evening from the forests of the big city. From the very first day I had been hurt and puzzled by his indifference and pessimism. Surely it couldn't be that he resented my preoccupation and present priorities? Where had that young police inspector gone who used to stop his car in order to ferry jay-walking hedgehogs and toads to safety in his cap? Had the passing years so hardened him?

'I knew you would be disappointed and I didn't want you to be hurt. The longer they lived the worse it would be. I just didn't want you upset.'

Me the comforter now. 'It's all right. It was only a gamble anyway. I just wanted to see if I could solve the problem that seems to get hand-reared finches. It was all for science really.' Liar.

13

Difficult Days

After the previous day's medication I was hoping to see some improvement and my disappointment was all the greater when I could detect none. The writing in the diary for that day had deteriorated to a pencilled scrawl:

> 7 a.m. Antibiotic. No improvement. Cannot stand or swallow properly.
> 8.45 More difficulty swallowing. Not much taken.
> 11 a.m. Tried to feed greenflies. Difficulty swallowing.

Throughout the day I miserably reported the situation to enquiring family and friends. There was much sage nodding and 'Ah well, that's the way of it, isn't it?'

But from Yveline, 'Don't worry so much. The antibiotic takes time to be effective.' That night the last entry in the diary was in ink and read:

> Not too hopeful.

I felt as I wrote it, that although it was true, if I actually put it down on paper, it would have the effect that cleaning the car on a sunny day has – hail or rain within the hour. Or, conversely, lumber oneself with mac and brolly and the sun will shine all day.

I telephoned Viv, the bird-seed buyer, and she gave me some extraordinary advice, garnered from many years' experience with caged birds. The gist of it was that the bird must not be allowed to slip into a trough of despondency. Must not be allowed to take the easy sleepy way out. In her words:

'Jolly it along. Keep at it all the time. Make it fight.' My tender diffidence and reluctance to distress or cause pain was having no effect one way or the other. Nothing would be lost by trying. On reflection it made sense; after all, it worked for humans. The mental state was very important.

Late that night when we were in bed, the telephone rang. Henry: 'Have you tried the London Zoo or the Vet College at Brookmans Park?'

It was quite touching how many people were rooting for that little bird. It had to live. Was it really only fifteen days since our placid lives had been disrupted? Stay alive overnight, Squeaker, and I'll jolly you along on the morrow.

The first thing I noticed on the morrow was that one of Squeaker's eyes was not so glazed and although he was difficult to feed (egg and greenfly), he was trying to move. Awful though he looked, it was an improvement at last. Later that day, having spent most of the time in my hand or jumper subjected to lots of jolly chat and encouragement, he even tried to squeak. Possibly in annoyance, but that was a step in the right direction.

I had not realized how we had become accustomed to the really rather loud noises Squeaker used to make. How, in fact, without being conscious of it, I had learned to understand and interpret the many differing ejaculations. Now it seemed so quiet.

I feared his legs were paralysed and tested them on the perch. He would have fallen had I not been holding him but his legs did move.

Yveline said, 'Of course he is alright. You would feel dull and stupid after all those drugs.'

By 7.45 p.m. that evening he was able to perch and could make quiet cheeps. He was eating voraciously and seemed more co-ordinated. Could it be the worst was over?

On the next day he was doing so well that I put him out by himself in the garden. He still could not fly or move very well so I put the fireguard – not exactly a gilded cage – over him in case of crows or cats. We decided to stop the hit-and-miss dosing with the dog antibiotic as at this stage Squeaker was improving so rapidly and I feared that the drug side-effects would be harmful.

On the next day (Friday already!) Squeaker seemed to be slipping back and I rang the vet only to be told that the antibiotic must be administered for five days. Another two days to go. I should have remembered from my experience with the childrens' various ailments. It was terrible to watch the poor bird deteriorate that day despite medication and my guilt was multiplied.

Squeaker's rear toes were twisted under the feet and emerged upsidedown through the front toes. Just like the feet of dead birds. One eye had become sunken and glazed and he rocked unsteadily on his little twisted stumps.

It was Friday the thirteenth of July. The day that Yveline's husband Henry was whisked off to hospital by ambulance in screaming pain with an injured back.

Squeaker fed quite well that day despite his ghastly symptoms, which is more than could be said for poor Henry.

The next day Squeaker's back toes were still curled under and the one eye was still glazed and sunken. Henry was under heavy sedation in Highgate.

'Look, Yveline,' I said, 'with all those medicos running around, Henry is in an ideal situation to make some enquiries when he comes round. The first thing he must do is to ask if one of them knows anything about sick birds.'

It being Saturday, Harry was home and we spent all day playing with Squeaker and trying to prize his toes open so that he could perch on a finger. On Sunday morning the last dose of the antibiotic was given. It's up to you now, Squeaker, I thought. The invalid diet that day comprised: ant eggs, chopped gentles, a young grasshopper, caterpillars, greenfly, skinned and cooked broad bean, double cream, crushed peanut, blackfly, froghoppers, a crumb of cooked fish and soaked bread.

Squeaker became quite lively but as soon as he tried to hop, the back claws folded forward and he fell over. He made no attempt to fly and the wings drooped down.

14

A Stupid Accident

Day twenty-one. Three weeks old. If it had not been for the illness I would have expected Squeaker to have been flying well and finding some food for himself by now. I noticed that the other fledgling was looking very mature now, but it was still expecting tit-bits from the gang.

When could I safely wean Squeaker from his high-protein diet to more easily obtainable seeds and cereals which is what the adults were supposed to eat? The Layers' mash (ground mixed cereals) was still his least favourite food. The soft tweet of annoyance when it was offered was very similar to the tweet of satisfaction when a favourite such as scrambled egg or froghopper was produced. The nuances of difference in the sound would probably be unnoticed by an outsider, but the expression on the face would certainly make clear the meaning. A sulky closing of the eyes and turning the head away in the former case and eager sparkling eyes and urgent open beak in the latter.

Although the claws, voice and wings did not improve, the mental processes did not seem impaired. Today he was learning to peck from my finger and as he hopped and fell over the lawn he started to peck at (invisible to me) objects in the grass.

The sunken eye looked back to normal now so I began to test his eyesight. I found minute little caterpillars, less than an eighth of an inch long, hiding inside the buds at the top of the hairy willow herb plants that grew round the edge of the fish pond. I used to pick the whole tip of the plant off and pull open a bud so that the caterpillar could just be seen by a faint movement, then I would proffer the whole plant tip of several buds to Squeaker. Quick as a flash and with unerring accuracy the poor unfortunate delicacy was winkled out of its hiding-place. Sometimes I would hide crumbs or cheese in my fingernails to train him to seek out food for himself. My poor fingernails were now permanently stained dark greeny brown by their constant immersion in cuckoo spit – the sap sucked by the froghoppers. Also by now Squeaker's beak had become brown and pointed although still soft and yellow at the edges.

I remembered a time before E.T. died when I had taken the birds out for some exercise. Squeaker began gasping and I really thought he was about to die. When I picked him up I could see in the bright sunlight that both nostrils were blocked with rapidly drying food. As soon as the little holes were scraped clear all was well. It was in fact a narrow escape because if the light had not been so good or I had not taken them outside, I would never have noticed the cause of the trouble. I always made sure their faces were clean after that.

Squeaker began to wean himself. I need not have worried. The following day he refused worms and took a great fancy to wet white bread.

At this time I kept him in a nest in a box in the kitchen overnight but during the day he was outside. I had to keep constant observation as he could not fly and was not very strong. I imagined all sorts of horrors befalling him, ranging from falling into the fish pond to being pounced upon by a cat. As soon as it cooled in the evenings I brought him in and he liked to play around our necks as we sat on the sofa watching the television or talking. When it was dark outside and all the birds were roosting and quiet, Squeaker would cat nap in our collars then run round our chests or backs to cheep softly and confidentially into an ear. I often wondered how he knew that those large fleshy things were organs of hearing. Most likely it was coincidence which brought him to the correct spot for his most intimate mutterings to be heard. Or had he quickly learned that there would be no answer or response if he were elsewhere and we did not hear? He still enjoyed putting his beak into my lips even though he was perfectly capable of drinking from a spoon. If it had not been for our worry about his future that would have been a most happy period.

A few days later when I went to the kitchen sink for some water for him he became so excited by the spoon that he leapt out of my hand right into the sink. That day, the sink, which is old and deep, was filled with a strong bleach solution. Don't panic, don't panic. I gasped in terror as I forced myself into a sensible sequence of events. Grab out the bird and turn on the mixer tap. Test for temperature. We don't want scalds as well as bleach burns. Inundate the already half drowned bird and rinse and rinse. And how about pulling out the plug in case you drop it again? For one who was a fairly voiceless convalescent, Squeaker put up a good show of hysteria and fight. When I judged the bleach was off his body I licked and licked his eyes until all taste and smell of bleach had gone. Poor Squeaker, all his fine feathers wet and clinging revealing his original gangling bony shape and long neck and a great deal of unfledged pink skin.

By good fortune I was wearing a towelling T-shirt, one of his favourites, so I popped him under it and he snuggled into my bra and stayed there for two hours. I occasionally breathed hot air down the neck hole to speed the drying process.

Whilst he was quiet and now out of harm's way, I decided to telephone a woman whose name had been given to me by someone who knew that she kept birds. Perhaps she had experience of the side-effects of antibiotic? Did it weaken the wings and distort the feet?

Despite being called in the middle of her lunch, Beryl seemed most sympathetic. What she thought about my incompetence in dropping my charge into a sink full of bleach I don't know. However we warmed to each other and although she could offer no advice regarding my sparrow she promised to let me know if she found out anything.

We met several times after that and she had many interesting stories of bird behaviour to relate.

A STUPID ACCIDENT

Once an injured pigeon was brought to her back door. It was put in a box by the boiler and fed. After three days it perked up and was taken via the back door to the front garden for some exercise and fresh air. It hopped around for a while and then made straight for the front porch, through the front door, turned right along the hall, into the kitchen and into the box by the boiler. It had never seen the front of the house nor the hall before, but it knew exactly where to go.

Beryl also told me of a blackbird she had tamed and which was very fond of cheese. One day when sitting on her chair in the porch, Beryl offered cake instead and hid the cheese in a plastic bag under a cushion. As soon as her back was turned the clever bird had found the cheese and opened the bag.

Sadly he was run over by a car whilst waiting for her to return one day.

This was one of the reasons I had never been keen to tame a wild bird. Delightful though their activities are when they show no fear of humans, it is a rather unnatural existence and their craven reliance on fickle humans could lead to their downfall. What happens when the provider falls ill, goes on holiday or moves?

John Clare (1793–1864), the peasant poet, tamed a sparrow which had a similar sad end:

The common sparrow is well known but not so much in a domesticated state as few people think it worth while bringing up a sparrow. When I was a boy I kept a tamed cock sparrow 3 years. It was so tame that it would come when called and flew where it pleased. When I first had the sparrow I was fearful of the cat killing it, so I used to hold the bird in my hand toward her and when she attempted to smell of it I beat her. She at last would take no notice of it and I ventured to let it loose in the house. They were both very shy of each other at first, and when the sparrow ventured to chirp, the cat would brighten up as if she intended to seize it but she went no further than a look or smell. At length she had kittens and when they were taken away, she grew so fond of the sparrow as to attempt to caress it. The sparrow was startled at first but came to by degrees and ventured so far at last as to perch upon her back. Puss would call for it when out of sight like a kitten and would lay mice before it the same as she would for her own young. They always lived in harmony, so much so that the sparrow would often take away bits of bread from under the cat's nose and even put itself in a posture of resistance when offended as if it reckoned her no more than one of its kind. In winter when we could not bear the door open to let the sparrow come out and in, I was allowed to take a pane out of the window, but in the spring of the third year my poor Tom Sparrow – for that was the name he was called by – went out and never returned. I went day after day calling out for Tom and eagerly eyeing every sparrow on the house, but none answered the name, for he would come down in a moment to the call and perch upon my hand to be fed. I gave it out that some cat which it mistook for its old favourite betrayed its confidence and destroyed it.

At least one hundred and eighty years have passed since that event but how it brought back the morning when Squeaker was lost and too young to fend for himself. How I too called and called in vain and eagerly eyed the other small sparrow on the lawn. John Clare's father was a simple labourer and the story goes to show just how that Tom Sparrow must have won a place in his heart for permission to be given to remove a pane of glass from the window in the winter. Little did I guess at this time the alterations that I was to consider and the additions I made to our house in just the same cause.

15

Froghoppers

Day twenty-eight. Squeaker was eating voraciously but still showed a preference for egg, insects and bread. He also ate cooked rice and potato. Mother said that her gang of sparrows waited eagerly for her leftover porridge every morning, so I offered that too. I knew that given a wide choice, Squeaker, like many a human counterpart, would just go for the 'junk' food. His real favourite was wet white sliced bread closely followed by softened sweet biscuits.

He was looking mature and was mentally very alert. Every day I exercised his feet. I forced the curled toes of one foot open, clamped them onto my left forefinger and held them in place with the left thumb. Then, very much against his wishes, I tackled his other foot. By the time I had unfurled it I found that I needed a third hand to hold it onto the perch. I persevered, however, as I was afraid of the tendons shortening. I also encouraged him to hop along the ground as, left to his own devices, he was quite happy to squat like a duck in the middle of the lawn. A sitting duck, I feared. So I put him down on the ground about three feet away from me and I knelt down in front of him and called, 'Come on, Squeaker, come on. I know you can do it. Good Squeaker. Come, come to me.'

That morning Melvin, the milkman, had been watching this performance as Squeaker kept falling flat on his face as he hopped and hobbled towards my outstretched hands.

'He looks a goner to me.'

'Oh no, *no*. You don't realize, he has improved no end. He's doing very well.'

Melvin looked sceptical as well he might, then as we chatted he said something that was very true. He was not surprised that all my enquiries about sparrow health had come to nought: after all, most people were not very interested in sparrows or their survival, were they?

John Clare, my previously quoted poet, was. He wrote a poem called 'To Boys not to kill the Sparrows on his Roof'.

> Sure my sparrows are my own,
> Let ye then my birds alone.
> Come poor birds from foes severe
> Fearless come, you're welcome here:
> My heart yearns at fate like yours,
> A sparrow's life's as sweet as ours.

He goes on to excuse their theft of grain which he says is forced upon them by hunger and to remark that had they not eaten the pests from growing crops, there might be none to reap at all.

That day Squeaker showed a very marked interest in the gang on the back lawn, watching them feed and bathe.

In the afternoon, when I called for him, he hobbled and ran towards me from the lower lawn. Oh dear, this was dangerous territory for a young bird. The fish pond, wide areas of grass, shrubs and trees where he could get lost or wander into the neighbours' gardens. It seemed that despite his inability to fly and use his feet properly, he was becoming more mobile.

The next morning he was loudly chirruping for breakfast just like old times. At last he had his proper voice back. Now, perhaps, his feet and wings would improve.

He was spending the whole day in the garden now; hopping and falling from a favourite rockery stone to perch on the hose pipe which was on the ground or shelter under a plant. I fed him almost every hour but I noticed that he was becoming much more wary. Even of me. When I appeared he would run happily towards me, then suddenly, when he was about ten feet away, he would stop and look puzzled. Then he would start displacement activities: yawning, pretending to preen or defecating. Could it be that the gang had communicated their fear of humans to him? I was tempted into an anthropomorphism,

'Oh goody, there's my Mum. Oh *no*, hang about, they said she's enemy No. 1. What the blazes do I do now?'

Poor little bird, psychological problems to contend with as well.

Day thirty. He was still chirruping well and at 8 a.m., after his breakfast, I put him outside. At 10 a.m. he came when I called but was far too nervous to be picked up so I fed him from my finger. Now obviously was the time to stop being so possessive. It must be his decision when to come. I must let him call the tune. Which he sensibly did – loudly at the back door. In the evening, of course, I brought him into the house as usual.

A friend came to lunch the next day and before she had time to put her handbag down, she was whisked off to the woods for a froghopper hunt.

Yveline and I had long since cleared all the main paths and clearings of the sort which hung on the bushes. Those on the grass were small and pale yellow or white. As their 'spit' seemed to be stickier, it was hardly worth bothering to bend low to extract them.

Those at waist height on the blackberries were best, larger and green or pinky brown. The only snag was that it was rather painful extracting them from the prickly stems. Yveline's finger-nails being long and strong saved her fingers but the little creatures had a habit of getting under the nails. So instead of my handy rhythm: dive, blow, tap, snap, wipe, with her it was: dive, blow, scrape out, tap, etc.

We noticed that, as the days went by, those that had escaped our darting eyes had grown rather large and were getting gregarious. As many as six could be found huddled together under their foam duvet. We could always tell when there would be more than one hidden because the 'spit' would have a skin over it. This must be the short resting, or pupa, stage.

As this little insect played such an important and sacrificial role in this story, it is worthwhile describing its own interesting life cycle. One of the commonest is called *Philaenus spumaria*, belonging to the order of the plant bugs.

In autumn the mother froghopper, an active insect almost half an inch long, lays her eggs in the deep crevices of the bark of bushes or similar and soon afterwards dies. The eggs hatch in the spring and the little green larvae emerge. The body is flat below and pointed behind, with a head bent down upon the breast and with the usual three pairs of legs well suited to taking a firm grip of the plants. Like all its relatives, it has a piercing and sucking proboscis which it presses into the stem of a plant. It gets such a rich supply of sugary sap that it overflows. Along the underside of its body there is a runnel in which air can be held, and the froghopper works its body up and down until the captured air gets thoroughly mixed up with the surplus sap which passes out of the food canal. Rather like whisking egg white for meringues. As it does this, a little wax is added from glands on the skin and a little ferment from the food canal. If it were just sap bubbles it would soon disappear in the heat of the day, but, being something like soap, it lasts, and keeps the young insect moist; very few enemies will touch the frothy mass.

The insect grows and moults and grows and moults again. Finally it passes into a resting or pupa stage; its wings grow, and other changes of structure are brought about. It leaves the froth and moults for the last time, then it becomes a full-grown winged insect.

I was sorry to sacrifice them as they had gone to so much trouble, but my bird came first.

This day my visitor and I were forced to search out the smaller ones clinging to the grass. There were not so many of those left now either and I wondered if our relentless depredation would alter the ecology of this woodland in some minor way.

The next day bountiful nature came to the rescue in two ways. First a neighbour, who was just off on holiday, donated a small aquarium acrawl with newly hatched stick insects, and secondly the heavy weather brought forth a swarm of flying ants.

16

A Turning Point

A new worry was looming on the horizon. In less than a month we were due to go abroad. As Squeaker could not fly properly and had to be brought in at night for his own health and safety, he was still very dependent.

I decided it was time he learned to compete for some of his food, so I scattered the white bread for the gang as well. I noticed another gang of sparrows were having a fine old time on my seed beds in the kitchen garden. I would not need to do much thinning out of seedlings as every six inches or so the fine soil was scraped into shallow depressions for their dust baths. As Squeaker's activities were mainly confined to the upper lawn, I made him his own dust bath in a tray. I used dry orange builders' sand. He soon got the hang of it and it afforded him hours of pleasure. He spent so much time playing in it that his feathers became quite yellow from the sand and he was easy to spot in a crowd at a distance. I also fixed up a low water bath for him so that he could find his own drink and bathe as often as the others did in high containers or the fish pond.

Day thirty-four. At last he began to essay small flights and I was overjoyed when he perched in the rhododendrons with the other sparrows.

The next day he was very lively and fluttering, interrupting my telephone conversations by squeaking loudly into the handset. In the afternoon he actually caught a winged ant for himself.

By now when the gang came down onto the lawn to forage, my little limping bird used to try to join them. He had taken a great fancy to the largest cock sparrow. Dad? When this bird was on the lawn Squeaker hopped and hobbled to position himself in front of it about six inches away. He was totally ignored and if he went any closer the cock flew off, which seemed to be a signal to the rest of the gang who followed suit leaving the earthbound Squeaker alone and disconsolate.

I felt just as a mother does when her child is the only one left over when sides are being picked for team games. Never mind, Squeaker, at least you'll get first pick of all the goodies if I have anything to do with it.

The next day was the first of August and after the usual evening with us, I took Squeaker up to our bedroom when we went to bed. We had several very large indoor plants in the room and one, *Rhoiycissus rhomboidea*, was on a tall pedestal and was thick and twiggy and a suitable perch. Ideal for weaning him out of his box at night. Eventually, and before we went on holiday, I hoped to have him roosting outside at night, and this would be a stepping-stone. When he was used to the plant, I could put the whole thing outside under the loggia.

Two days later he was quite accustomed to perching at night on the plant. In the mornings he swooped down and crash-landed onto the duvet.

The third morning I was awoken by a soft wing brushing my cheek and the quietest of cheeps in my ear. The sensation afforded me indescribable pleasure, and the following morning, although I was first awake, I pretended to be asleep and awaited with joy my little bird's greeting.

We soon fell into a happy routine. As soon as I had despatch-ed the humans, I returned to bed with Squeaker's and my breakfast on a tray. When we had both finished, I took him downstairs on my shoulder to the lawn where he played the clinging infant for a while. As I put up my hand to dislodge him from one shoulder he ran round my back to the other. I put up my other hand and back he ran. Then I put up both hands at once and he ran down the centre of my back. Only when I started to jump up and down would he consent to get onto my hand whereupon I tossed him into the air. He usually managed to fly to the rhododendrons.

64

Bimbo's favourite chair was now permanently occupied
by the birds' paraphernalia.

Top E.T. and Squeaker about 8 days old.
Bottom Not yet ready to fly.

Top They often quarrelled with each other.
Bottom Two weeks old, flying and perching freely in the garden.

Harry spent all day trying to straighten Squeaker's toes.

Top Thirty days old and still unable to fly.
Bottom Squeaker, fifty days old, at his bird bath.

Top A favourite perch in the magnolia tree.
Bottom Squeaker in his private sand tray.

October.
Squeaker visiting Harry.

We enjoyed our living mobiles.

Top Partlet was too shy to come near.
Bottom Partlet in the kitchen searching for Squeaker.

His feet were much better now and although he could fly a little, his shape looked all wrong when he stood on the ground. My mother was the first to voice what I had refused to admit.

'He's not right, you know. His wings hang down too much. He needs a good dose of cod liver oil.'

Well, why not? I had some in the house. Although Squeaker did not like it, it seemed to herald the turning point of his recovery.

17

Lake Garda

During the following ten days Squeaker continued his slow improvement and I continued lacing his favourite food with cod liver oil.

His wings became stronger until he was flying high into trees and, to my constant worry, beyond reach in the dangerous and unknown territories outside our garden. He was still spending his nights on the potted plant indoors, however. Now in the mornings I launched him from the bedroom window. Unfortunately, as he still liked to play the clinging infant game, running round the back of my neck, I had to lean out rather a long way to dislodge him. He always flew across the back of the house to the top of a mature decorative crab apple tree outside Gemma's window, where he began to preen vigorously in the early morning sunlight. Invariably the juvenile that the Gang of Four used to feed joined him in the tree, perching about one foot away and also preening. One morning the juvenile was already in the tree and called to Squeaker as soon as I opened the window. For once Squeaker flew off my shoulder straight away.

As soon as Yveline's husband, Henry, was off his bed of pain, we dragged him round to admire Squeaker. As we stood that evening on the terrace, I found a cold and dead newly hatched nestling and I put it without a third thought into the compost bin. Squeaker's foolish parents still at it in the same nest. Just as well they were not too successful. The original Gang of Four had expanded to a canny gang of ten who had learned to imitate Squeaker's voice and congregate like hunched vultures in the crab apple tree whenever they heard me call. A robin and dunnock were also regular members of the copycat chorus.

I noted in the diary at this time that Squeaker was not doing so many displacement activities and seemed to find human v. bird loyalties easier to cope with. He seemed more confident with both. If only he could feed himself.

Day fifty and six more days before we went away. It was time to get Squeaker used to sleeping out at night. During the day I made preparations. I carried the enormous *Rhoiycissus rhomboidea* outside and rigged it high up under the loggia. At half-past nine that evening as dusk was blurring the edges of the bushes and all the garden birds had twittered their last good-nights, I fetched Squeaker and put him in it. I put the feather duster over him to be on the safe side.

At half-past six the next morning I rushed out to see how Squeaker had fared. He was still asleep! He enjoyed scrambled egg for breakfast and during the day discovered that the best way to dry off after a nice bath was to roll in the short hair at the back of my neck and the top of my collar (the trusty towelling T-shirt again).

The following morning was quite damp and foggy, and Squeaker was discovered with the gang in the crab apple tree. He flew down, but was reluctant to come in, and as soon as he had fed he flew off like a rocket to join the others.

The next day was wet and misty and he followed me round the house in the morning. In the afternoon I saw him pecking on the lawn with the gang, and that evening he found his own roost. In the wisteria that grew up a pillar of the loggia, I guessed.

Only two more days to go before 'D' day (departure day). I

had pinned to the utility room wall a large chart with the roster of volunteers who would be coming throughout the day to make sure my foster bird did not starve. Gemma would take over at the weekends. There were also lists of telephone numbers to call in various emergencies and standby volunteers in case Gemma, Yveline, Gladys or Fred should be struck down by some unforeseen event or illness and not be able to cater for my bird.

On that penultimate day Squeaker heard my voice in the front garden talking to a tradesman. He flew over the roof and onto my head. I felt some explanation of this wondrous and unusual (to the outsider) event was called for so I casually remarked that the bird knew me as I had reared it from birth.

'Oh yes,' said my unastonished visitor, 'as I was saying, those pipes will be well silted up by now.'

'Have you ever seen one like this before?' I persisted.

'What is it? A sparrow?'

'Yes.'

'Well of course I've seen them before.'

The last day I tried to leave Squeaker as much as possible to his own devices but that contrary bird came into the utility room, through the kitchen and into the hall where he stood at the foot of the stairs calling me down.

Lake Garda was lovely as usual but this time I was preoccupied. As I gathered wild flowers on our long walks I also scoured the verges and hillsides for ripe succulent grass seeds which I then carefully packed in my suitcase. Other guests at the hotel were quizzed on their knowledge of bird illness until finally my spouse expostulated in exasperation,

'Promise that you will get through the next meal without dragging that bloody bird into the conversation.'

We decided to telephone home the very next morning for news. Gemma laconically replied, 'Oh, it's you. Yes, yes, the bird is still around. Everyone else is OK too, actually.'

We missed Squeaker and found that we noticed the sparrows all around us now. Harry always saved a breakfast roll to crumble on our balcony for the scruffy little hotel gang that we had never been aware of on previous visits. It had always been the musical blackcap in the gardens that we searched out first.

One day as we picnicked on the peninsular of Sirmione we watched a very smart band of Italian sparrows, all black and chestnut, bathing at the water's edge and I wondered if they could possibly be the descendants of Catullus' sparrow who danced and sang. Caius Valerius Catullus (87–54 B.C.), the Latin lyric poet who established a new form of literature in Rome and is probably best known for his love poems to Lesbia, was supposed to have lived just a few yards from where we sat.

> Sparrow, my Lesbia's darling pet,
> Her playmate whom she loves to let
> Perch in her bosom and then tease
> With tantalising fingertips,
> Provoking angry little nips . . .

After the sparrow's death Catullus tells how Lesbia mourned:

> Graces and cupids, weep and gather near,
> Weep, all ye mortals that love lovely things:
> Dead is the darling sparrow of my Dear.
> More than her eyes she loved him. Sweet was he.
> As a maid knows her mother he knew her,
> And never was he fain to quit her knee.
> Yet he would flutter round and pipe his lay:
> For he alone piped, his sovereign Queen.
> Now must he fare along the sunless way,
> Now must he journey to that dwelling dim
> Whence – as too well men know – none comes again.
> Woe upon Orchus' night that ravished him!
> Alas, poor little sparrow, for whom being dead
> My Dear has wept until her eyes are red.

Two thousand years ago a woman wept for her sparrow and I

worried now lest Orchus' night should ravish my Squeaker before we returned.

Several dozen ice creams later, as Harry unpacked the car, I rushed round into the back garden.

Gladys and Fred were standing under the magnolia tree holding up a polythene ice cube container of millet, and a little brown bird with three black feathers on his breast was perched on a branch vigorously pecking it up.

'Squeaker, I'm back!'

He lifted his head and stared for an instant, then resumed the far more important activity of filling his crop.

The three black feathers showed that he was in fact a male bird and I was delighted to know that my instinct had been sound. That evening we heard how Squeaker had trained my helpers over the past two weeks.

He would allow no undue familiarity and no one had been able to touch him; not even Yveline. He required the food to be put into the ice cube containers and proffered up to his special perch in the magnolia. Moreover, if anyone was ten minutes late or ten minutes early, he would not appear until the correct time however long they called. When he had had enough to eat he would give a short chirp and fly off. Gladys liked to think that it was a 'thanks and cheerio', but I knew better. I noticed that most sparrows made the same quick noise as they flew off a perch, especially on an upward or level trajectory. When flitting downwards they often did not. Prosaically, it would seem that it was nothing more nor less than a grunt of effort in much the same way as certain tennis players vocalize as they serve a ball.

The next day was Sunday and all morning Squeaker came at various intervals to accept seeds and insects from the containers. He treated me politely but distantly like a stranger. That's what I wanted, wasn't it? As soon as I was sure that he could find his own food I would have successfully finished my assignment, wouldn't I?

But what about my little friend and our communication and the games?

After lunch I sat on the wall of the rockery and started talking to the little bird perched in the magnolia tree. Suddenly he flew down onto my shoulder and started to peck my ear quite sharply. He then attacked my cheek and as I turned my face to him, he put his beak into my mouth in the old confiding way. I snatched up some millet and he hopped onto my hand to eat it. Instead of flying off when he had finished it, he pecked and pulled at my hands and fingers until he had arranged them into a comfortable nest shape. He then sank down onto his haunches for a snooze.

I was uncomfortable sitting like a bemused statue on the stone, so I carefully carried him to the loggia where I found a softer perch for myself in a deckchair. We stayed like that together for exactly half an hour. He had never done such a thing before, nor has he since. As he slept in my hands a crow flew overhead and cawed. Squeaker jumped up ready to fly for cover then looked round at me and sank back on his haunches once more and closed his eyes.

When he flew off I found that I had missed the whole of 'Gardeners' Question Time' on the radio, and I didn't mind a bit.

18

Some Precedents

The next morning on returning from a long walk in the woods with a group of local birdwatchers, we congregated on my front drive for a chat. Squeaker must have heard my voice amongst the others for he flew right over the house and straight down onto my head where I stood in the centre of seven similarly clad birdwatchers. I had not called him and our voices were at a normal pitch. The front garden was not his familiar patch either.

I was flattered that he had singled me out so unerringly, but remembered Beryl's blackbird who was run over by a car as he waited for her.

During the next few days Squeaker taught me his new habits. His favourite food was now peeled sunflower seeds, and if I was a bit slow getting the cases off, he would give my finger a sharp peck. He did not like to come into the house in the mornings, even if it meant that I became rather chilled feeding him outside. Nor did he care for a certain pink outfit I once wore. I had long since given up wearing my gold chain round my neck or any form of earrings. They seemed to make him quite angry and his attempts to remove them caused me many an inadvertent nip. As I had also given up perfume, had rather stained fingernails and invariably wore garments that Squeaker deemed suitable, it occurred to me that I was beginning to look a bit like a sparrow myself.

Why did I suffer this little despot? Well, he wasn't really. He certainly thought of me as his protector and acted just like a baby when scared. He did not like me to leave him when he was feeding because as soon as my back was turned, the robin took over with the greedy gang waiting in the wings. Little Squeaker came last in their pecking order. Besides, I wanted to fatten him up well before winter.

Once as I came unexpectedly into the utility room from the kitchen, there was a mad panic of wings for the exit and crashings against the windows. Squeaker amongst them. As soon as he saw me he rushed to my shoulder for protection against this human monster that had frightened them. Many times when anyone other than Harry made overtures towards him, he would fly with a loud squawk straight for the comfort of my neck.

When it was cold or wet I used to feed Squeaker as I sat on a chair in the utility room. I wondered whether, like John Clare, I should remove a pane of glass from the window as winter approached so that he could come in by himself. Or perhaps a miniature cat-flap in the door? Something would have to be done before winter. If I left food out for Squeaker the others rushed down first and then the bigger birds were attracted. As it was, the robin and gang of ten all swarmed into the room as soon as my back was turned. I eventually made a little porch so that the rain would not come in when I left the door ajar Squeaker size.

No such problems beset Clara Beasley, a maid in service with a Mrs Hervey of Beechfield, Alderly Edge in Cheshire who wrote to *Country Life* in 1901:

> We were going for a walk one evening last July, when Miss Marjorie found a tiny bird lying on the ground close to the house. It had evidently just been hatched, and must have fallen from a considerable height, as the nearest nest was in a pipe which runs round the roof of the house. We decided to keep it and, having gained permission from Mrs Hervey to do so, we found a quill, fed our pet with bread and milk, and placed it in a nest of cotton wool. We did not then think it could possibly live many minutes. Our astonishment was therefore very great to find, when we returned from our walk, that it was not only alive but very bright, and quite satisfied with its surroundings.

> I took it to my room that night and, in answer to its cries, fed it two or three times during the night. From that time it grew very quickly, and could hop and fly short distances, being covered with a little coat of brown feathers, and so betraying that he came of very common parentage. But the word common could not be applied to our wee birdie. From the very first day he was with us he carefully studied our words and the expressions of our faces, and soon grew to understand both, and, from the day he could fly about, entered into every detail of our human life with an energy and intelligence that at times would startle us, so very unnatural did it seem to us.

When the room was warm, birdie was most particular about his bath, and was so vain that he would not show himself until his little coat was dry and neatly arranged.

Birdie's chief point of observation was from my shoulder. Often when sewing he would fly to my finger and, holding the point of the needle in his tiny beak, endeavour to draw it from the work and, failing this, would set to work to pull out all the previous stitches. He would fly away with needles, buttons and hooks, and carefully hide them. He soon learnt his way about the house and when we went to any of the rooms would quickly come in search of us and, on finding us, would fly to our shoulders, fluttering his little wings and chirping with great pleasure and excitement.

He was extremely fond of lace and jewellery, and would critically examine any new thing, expressing either approval or disgust. Often he would stand over a thing and fight most bravely for its possession, even keeping three of us at bay; and often at meals would eat from our plates, but would eat nothing laid upon the table-cloth.

We have a canary in the nursery, which whistles most sweetly, and so well could birdie imitate him that not the slightest difference could be detected. He soon changed his first coat of feathers for a very pretty one – it was a very glossy shaded brown, with grey and black breast and grey feathers on either side. Birdie managed to fly away through the nursery window three times, twice returning of his own accord after being away two hours. But the third time, after sitting near the window for some time, he flew away to the orchard, and when night came he had not returned, and our efforts to find him were in vain.

Early the next morning I went down to the orchard, and called him by name, when to my great astonishment he flew to my shoulder, and expressed the greatest delight at being found.

Birdie's death occurred on January 13th. The children and I

were playing with a toy train, and as usual birdie came to give us his assistance. How the accident occurred, no one can say but, chancing to turn a moment, we saw our wee pet stagger and fall. Carefully we raised him, but all our efforts to save him were in vain; in three minutes he died.

Throughout his life he never expressed the slightest fear, and so in the last moments he gave no sign of the pain through which he passed, only when the brief struggle was over raised his tiny head, gave us one last bright look, as though he fully realised our deep sorrow, and with one cry of farewell fell back lifeless. Birdie, our sweet little companion, was gone, and all that remains to us are the sweetest memories and a silent little figure, which now stands on a cabinet in the nursery, watching with calm indifference all those actions which once could not have proceeded without his tiny help.

How that story reminded me of Squeaker and the love such a bird, even one 'of very common parentage', can inspire. The main difference is, of course, that mine is a free bird and theirs was kept as a pet indoors all the time.

When Squeaker was fed entirely by me and before he had joined the gang, he loved to play and be entertained and, had it been my intention, I'm certain I could have taught him many tricks and activities the normal bird has no time to pursue. It would seem that diet was not such an important feature in successful rearing as I had imagined. But at least I had discovered why, if sparrow nestlings were not exposed to the cold too long before they were found, they were uninjured by their great 'falls' to the ground.

Many months later I heard of another successful raising of a newly hatched nestling. This one was found by Clare Kipps in 1940 and the story of its long life, 12 years, 7 weeks and 4 days, is told in her book, *Sold for a Farthing*.

Owing to a slight deformity this bird was never allowed a free life, but perfectly adapted itself to living with a human and was

Mrs Kipps's constant companion and friend. This bird, too, learned to sing and could also do card tricks in front of an audience and entertained many people during the worst of the London Blitz.

I soon began to realize, to my comfort, that my obsession, which I now freely admitted, was not so unusual after all.

So, back to our muttons – Squeaker.

Halfway through September I took temporary charge of my daughter Lois and her husband Ray's gentle cockatiel, Pina Colada, and Snowflake, a bad-tempered budgerigar.

'Don't let that mangy little bird of yours near them, I don't want mine to catch anything,' instructed my elder daughter. 'You know all wild birds have parasites, don't you? By the way, has Robbie (Bimbo) been wormed lately? You don't do it nearly often enough.'

'Goodbye dears, have a lovely holiday,' I interposed. That week Bimbo had a bad time coping with three birds instead of one, but worse was to follow.

19

The Sick Bay

I did not know it at the time but was told later by an expert that one of the noises I made to call Squeaker was very attractive to the family *Mustelidae*. In other words, every time I pursed my lips tightly and drew in air to make the familiar squeaking noise, any polecat, ferret, stoat, marten or weasel that was in the vicinity would be drawn to me. And that is how Ferdy joined the menagerie.

One morning as I stood at the back door calling Squeaker for breakfast, a small dark brown animal came lolloping and limping round the house from the front garden. I had no idea what it was but could guess from the look of its bared teeth that it was no friend of a sparrow. Nor human probably. But it had come to me and must be in a dire state to do so. First I fetched a large cardboard box with a lid, then I put on Harry's heavy leather gardening gloves and gingerly approached my visitor.

'Oh go away now, Squeaker, be quiet, Pina Colada, not *now*, Bimbo.' Then I urged the little animal (about the size of an elongated grey squirrel) into the box and put it under the shelter of the loggia. I fetched a raw egg and some water and it sucked and slurped up the egg in seconds. Then I emptied the potatoes out of their sack and put it in the box so that my guest could hide or sleep if it wanted to.

Was it a wild animal or someone's pet? I knew it wasn't a stoat or weasel, so I made out some postcards and pinned one on the blue cedar outside our house, one in the pet shop and one in the post office.

FOUND. BLACK FERRET/POLECAT?
Enquire within.

I can remember my first and last encounter with a ferret vividly, although it must be at least forty years ago. It was during the war when my mother kept some chickens at the bottom of the garden. One morning when I was despatched to fetch the eggs for breakfast, I pulled open the sliding wooden door of the chicken house and a scene of gory horror greeted my childish gaze. Headless birds all over the floor. Feathers and blood. As I crouched down to peer into the nest boxes to see if any hens were still alive, I came face to face with the bloodied perpetrator.

To this day I remember the snarling bared teeth that dripped with blood and the hot *red* eyes that were fixed on mine. The crouching menace was dressed in a creamy white fur coat. As I ran screaming back to the house, I felt that all evil was personified by those hot red eyes and blood-spurting bared teeth. I could not believe that such an animal existed. I was especially worried about it being white.

My father was away in the army and I thought that the creature would not have dared such depredation had he been at home. Later someone explained about albinos and that what I had seen was a ferret and that all ferrets had red eyes and white fur.

But this little chap had beautiful dark brown tipped fur and such a pretty face. Almost like a Walt Disney cartoon animal. Nevertheless I busied myself making a more substantial cage. The two wooden top risers of a spare beehive lined with newspapers and topped with a metal grid weighted down with two pound weights made a splendidly strong sick bay. I put the whole thing in the utility room, for sick this poor little creature obviously was. He/she had bad diarrhoea and even in this extremity dragged itself to the corner of the box in order not to make a mess.

I wrapped Ferdy (the ferret?) in an old jumper and put him into his new quarters with a dish of Bimbo's dog meat and a bowl of milk.

That evening, before the weary hunter had time to put his car into the garage, I called, 'Come quickly, guess what I've got.'

Harry rather took to Ferdy.

My social life was now confined to visitors to me. I had no time at all for gadding. My aunt called the next day and as we made a tour of inspection in the kitchen garden, I offered to cut her a cabbage. As I bent with the knife there was an awful scream and we both jumped back in fright. Not a sensitive cabbage to contend with now surely? No, of course not. The explanation limped away from us in the form of a frog with a torn and bleeding leg. Had we trodden on it by mistake? No, indeed, for coiled fatly under the cabbage was a mature grass snake which had been foiled of its dinner by our chance intervention.

Into a plastic bucket with the frog and up to the house. It only seemed a jaggy flesh wound so I slid it into a tiny pond (the old baby bath) on the rockery, which had plenty of moist resting places and lots of froggy foods.

Ferdy was deteriorating. His breathing was becoming very laboured and, despite ministrations with steaming oil of eucalyptus, did not improve. He then began to moan with a most human-like voice,

'Oh dear, Oh de-e-a-ar.' It was most weird. Just like a child. I wrapped him warmly in an old towel and took him upstairs to show to Gemma who lay in her sickbed with a high temperature and sore throat.

'Phone the vet,' she moaned.

Who for, I wondered, as I searched the rockery pond for the wounded frog.

The vets at Barnet decided to keep Ferdy in hospital for observation. I wanted all his bones checked too as he could have been run over on the road before he reached me. He was eventually diagnosed as suffering from pneumonia and suitable antibiotics were injected. After a few days the vet rang to say that Ferdy was well enough to be brought home. In fact, as he was so lively, he was upsetting the other patients. There were no broken bones and I could carry on with the medication in tablet form.

Harry and I were so pleased to have this pretty little creature back that we had failed to ask what sort of creature it was. Ferdy seemed quite tame, but I was not taking too many chances with those teeth. As the days went by he became very energetic indeed. As soon as I raised the metal grill on his makeshift cage, he was up and over the beehive risers like a liquid fur tippet and out and up and into the compost bin before you could say 'peelings'.

I made a tiny collar from a suede watch strap and took him for walks round the garden on Bimbo's lead. Poor puzzled Bimbo. To crown it all, Bimbo must have been aware that I was feeding this new interloper on *her* dog food laced with *extra* goodies such as chicken and egg.

When I put the miniature collar on for the first time, I found a piece of string tied tightly round our visitor's neck embedded in the fur. I also found several large sheep ticks firmly attached and swollen with the blood of my wobbly invalid. Ugh. Fortunately a pair of nail scissors soon dealt with the string and flea powder soon dealt with the ticks which all dropped off after two days.

Bimbo was utterly intrigued by this rather strong-smelling newcomer. I think she thought she might have a new playmate and ally against the steadily growing numbers of feathered things which so claimed my attention. She nosed closely behind as Ferdy darted from cover to cover. Ferdy did not like open spaces and kept close to plants or walls. I was not too sure that Bimbo would not attempt to treat him like her plastic toys, and, more to the point, I was even less sure of Ferdy's temper and teeth. So Bimbo was banished once more.

Squeaker still demanded four good meals a day and Pina Colada and Snowflake's cage was sorely in need of a good clean. Not to mention the humans' habitation. Being summer, however, I was able to disguise most of the squalor with very large and trailing flower arrangements. We usually ate outside in the evenings and Bimbo and Squeaker vied for the crumbs. The al fresco life suited all of us this fine September but I was very well aware that autumn and winter would be a very different bowl of millet.

I would have to find a good home for Ferdy. An adult who could look after him properly. No more sheep ticks and string.

Finally the perfect new owner was found. One day Yveline telephoned in great excitement. Henry's secretary's husband who worked with computers also kept ferrets! What an unlikely coincidence. But then Yveline and Henry were, on the surface, a seemingly unlikely pair of aiders and abetters in my sparrow-raising project. No khaki-clad wildlife buffs, they; more the elegant participants of an American soap opera. Yveline's knowledge of bird life was severely limited, but this winter had proved her to be the most diligent and dedicated carer. Being newly introduced to birds and having a mere sparrow, Squeaker, as her yardstick, all comers to her bird table were greeted with equal enthusiasm and unprejudiced generosity. Starlings were her favourites – after sparrows, of course. Henry's only previous brush with birds was probably on a plate between a knife and fork at a business lunch.

One or two children had been interested in Ferdy and wanted an unusual pet but I felt this was an animal for an adult and I did not want it to be someone's nine-day wonder either. After a good deal of research and hunting up telephone numbers of 'suitable' agencies or wild animal orientated people, I had had one or two very grudging offers to 'take it off your hands'. That was not what we wanted for Ferdy. Besides, he was still an invalid and needed special care. He enjoyed attention and I could not bear to think of him shut away in a cage forever.

I interviewed Alan, the secretary's husband, in the kitchen with Ferdy loose on the floor and Bimbo on my lap. I asked such pertinent questions as:

'I expect you spend a lot of time playing with your animals?'

'Er – um, I expect you have a very large run for them?'

And bluntly, 'How in fact would you treat him?'

All the questions were quite irrelevant for as soon as Ferdy approached Alan, her (she was a jill, he told me) whole attitude changed. She ran round and round the room gaily with her tail held erect and the fur splayed out on either side like a fan. She made strange excited squeakings. Look at me, look at me! Then ran to his hand for pretend boxing and biting games. I offered the leather gloves which were scornfully declined, 'No, no, she likes me and wants to play. She won't hurt me.' It was clearly love at first sight which appeared to be mutual. Alan already had two white ferrets which would be grand company and provide the warmth at night that these creatures seem to need. They all curl up together in the nest, he told me.

Ferrets are the domesticated albino form of polecat, it is thought. Ferdy would seem to be a cross between a polecat and a ferret. Alan told me that he had taught ferrets to play football with a ping pong ball and he handled them every day so that when he went hunting rabbits for the pot, the ferrets would want to come back to him. I was not sure about the hunting bit at first, but on reflection I realized that it would be a much more natural and healthy life for this hyper-active animal.

Good-bye Ferdy. Good luck.

The telephone rang that evening and a heavily disguised voice croaked, 'A three-legged elephant is limping up the hill towards your house and it has your address on a label round its neck.'

'Good night, Henry.'

20

A Very Handsome Bird

The only souvenir of Squeaker's illness or original fall was a useless left outer toe. It did not seem to hamper him in the least and I took great pride in his appearance. He was gradually growing a small black bib under his beak and a sweep of chestnut eyeshadow. The stripes on his back, which, incidentally, only cover the shoulders but appear longer because the wings carry on the theme, were in a definite pattern. Thin black stripes divide different distinct bands of colour. The centre panel which is the widest is speckled dark brown, fawn, grey, moss and many colours and tones in between. The panels on either side are completely different, each feather the same colour, a soft apricot. After the next dark stripe, the hazel speckled panel again. These outer two are partially covered by the wings. The back under the wings is a soft mossy grey. He still retained a little yellow at the edges of his beak and his overall colouring was not so strong as the other old males.

By the end of September he had acquired a new dark grey tail, each feather edged with brown. The yellow staining from the sand had disappeared and when I examined his sand bath on our return from holiday, I found that a cat had been using it as a urinal. I removed it entirely as the last thing I wanted to do was to encourage cats. The other juvenile sparrow had not changed colouring but had grown in size. A female then.

October came in with heavy thunderstorms. Poor craven Bimbo needed much comfort as from her behaviour I suppose she thought that with each flash of lightning the world was about to end. Now that the leaves were falling, where was poor Squeaker roosting? I know that, like some of the other sparrows, he perched at night on the leaf stalks of the Virginia creeper which clothes the back of the house in summer. But now, after a brief blaze of crimson and scarlet, the leaves relinquished their hold and fell like abandoned shields. Oh, Squeaker, where do you sleep now?

He came for food quite regularly but even in pouring rain would not linger too long in the house. One day as I sat feeding him in the utility room, I heard the telephone ring and I ran into the house to answer it with Squeaker still perched upon my shoulder. Just like the old days when he used to like joining in the conversations. But not for long. He was plainly unhappy in the hall and flew to the top of my head and jumped up and down making very restive tweets. I have noticed that when he flies to the top of Harry's or my head, it means that he wishes us to move in a certain direction, and if we do as we are told, he flies from perch to perch leading us. Usually to the utility room.

About this time I saw him round aggressively on another male who he thought was a contender for the food I was proffering. I was very pleased to see signs that he did not intend to stay last in the pecking order for ever. How the boot was on the other foot now. My handsome Squeaker flying to me confidently for his millet and sunflower seeds while the gang, who in the summer rejected him, now watched with jealous envy. I let them have the leavings. Often they were cravenly waiting in the crab apple tree for me to call Squeaker, who sometimes flew in from quite far afield.

By the end of the month he was independent enough to object to being lifted or offered a finger to get him out of a bush when he called to me. Sometimes it was just for a chat, but at other times it was to lead me to the soup kitchen which I had set up in the utility room. The soup kitchen was a 12" clay flowerpot set on a table with a twiggy shrub growing in it. Around the perimeter inside the lip of the pot I arranged the plastic ice cube containers each filled with a different delicacy and one filled with water. The routine was that I sat on the chair and Squeaker would swoop down through the outside door onto the plant. He would then drop down to the rim of the pot and hop around taking his pick. Then he would fly onto my hand which held the millet and finish off with that. I never tired of examining his plumage and features at close quarters; the colouring and patterning is so intricate and changing that it would take a book to describe it.

One cold damp day I had been out visiting and to combat the dreary weather had been lavish with my make-up and perfume spray. Squeaker was particularly friendly that afternoon when I returned and snuggled on my shoulder and played at putting his beak into my mouth. When he eventually flew off high over the oaks, I mused that he was probably the only sparrow flying around Hertfordshire smelling strongly of Chanel No. 5 and wearing bright pink lipstick.

Autumn and winter gardening chores were upon us now and one day as I stood in the garden in perfect peace with Squeaker on my shoulder, I heard my spouse in great impatience stamp up to the house and call,

'Where's Mummy, Gemma?'

And my charming daughter betrayed, 'Oh, she's in the garden with that soppy look on her face. Got the bird, I wouldn't wonder.' Out stomped the boots and scowl.

'I thought you were going to help with the compost heap twenty minutes ago.'

83

Then that clever bird flew to his head. It was as if a giant face flannel had wiped his face of all traces of ire and irritation and he sagged and smiled and wore his 'soppy' look. I sneaked off to the compost heap and let that lovely bird work its special magic.

November passed and as we sat snugly by the fire in the evenings, we often pondered on the past when a little bird once sat with us and played round our necks. Where was poor Squeaker shivering now? Each morning I was so relieved to see him swoop in for breakfast.

On December 16th, after a very wet night, I opened the back door and saw a dead sparrow at my feet. A male. *Passer domesticus*. A terrible calmness and numbness overcame me as I slowly bent to examine the cold wet body. I must behave like a grown up rational human being and not scream and scream with agony. Surely this bird was darker than Squeaker? Yes, but that's because it's soaking wet. Was Squeaker's white wing stripe quite so prominent?

Then there was a blessed swoosh of wings just brushing my hair and my dear, dear bird perched on the plant and stared at me with his bright, bright eyes.

As I popped the deceased into the compost bin I thought, one less old male for Squeaker to contend with in the spring.

21

The Eavesdropper

December, to our relief, was comparatively mild. Squeaker liked the routine of the soup kitchen. He preferred to land on the plant rather than me now and would allow no undue familiarity from anyone. A sharp admonitory peck would be the reward of a too enquiring finger.

Gladys and Fred (the holiday babysitters) called to see how Squeaker was faring. As we stood chatting by the back door, he flew down to a favourite perch in a standard rhododendron on the rockery. Just about eye level and ten inches or so beyond the average human arm reach. It was his favourite launching base for a flight through the slightly open back door and onto the plant of the soup kitchen. Gladys reached out to Squeaker who sidled rapidly down the twig to her hand for all the world like an infuriated crab. As soon as he was within reach he pecked viciously at her fingers. I would not have blamed her for thinking what a disloyal and ungrateful little beast Squeaker had become. And there was I gushing,

'Oh, see how fearless and bold he is. Did you ever see such bravery in a sparrow? I mean, he could just have flown off, couldn't he?'

I noticed that often he would fly straight out of the door in mid-feed in response to another sparrow's quiet call. Sometimes he responded by raising his head and giving a loud chirrup but continuing to perch on the hand which held the millet. When spring came and food was plentiful, would we ever see him again? Would we recognize him? The yellow on his beak had almost gone. It had often been suggested that I put a ring on his leg. I knew it was a commonplace habit in order to identify birds at a distance; lightweight different coloured plastic rings were used. The mere thought in connection with Squeaker horrified me. It would be an assault on his person. A betrayal of trust. An imposition and insult. Like branding property.

The diary notes over Christmas are brief:

> *Does not like Xmas cake.*
> *Does not like Xmas pudding.*

The real winter came on January 6th with the first snow. The pond and all the bird baths were frozen. By January 8th it was so cold that the water froze as soon as it was put out. I tried putting a little oily Vitapet in it to delay the process and distribute vitamins at the same time. I wish Squeaker would stay inside, but off he goes, goodness knows where, after each feed.

Once I saw him playing in the snow by the rhododendrons. He appeared to be having a dust bath and I was reminded of Thomas Hardy,

> A sparrow enters the tree.
> Whereon immediately
> A snow-lump thrice his own slight size
> Descends on him and showers his head and eyes,
> And overturns him
> And near inurns him.

Yveline, who, before the advent of Squeaker, took no notice of birds, now spent hours each day wading through the snow in her garden replenishing the bird tables with food and water. One such table on her terrace measures approximately four feet by two. She is thrilled and delighted with the mixed hoards it attracts. I gave her a field guide so that she can distinguish and name some of them. Indirectly, because of Squeaker, a great many birds have been saved from starvation this winter.

By January 22nd the snow had all gone and it was bright and sunny. On my way to the greenhouse I passed the rhododendrons and heard a loud *chur-churring*, and there was Squeaker hopping about in annoyance. Was he warning me off his territory? I turned back along the terrace and he followed me into the utility room. When I told Harry about it, he said that he had often noticed Squeaker in that area. Particularly on the gutter beneath our bedroom dormer window.

The following day the diary notes read,

January 23rd. Squeaker has a wife! Sparkling sunny day. Birds all singing. S on gutter 4ft. below bedroom window with long spray of pampas grass seed in mouth. Like white mustachioed Buddha. Followed female under tile into roof cavity.
January 24th. Observed female and S outside their nest. She sporting silver honesty seed pod. S still comes into house to be fed but chirrups

loudly outside nest. Rain. Gutter filling up and blocked. Must move blockage. 3.30 p.m. S indoors gorging. Wife outside snatching seed the greenfinch drops.

Well, there's a turn-up for the book. All winter when we worried and worried about the whereabouts of Squeaker, he was snugly ensconced under the roof, separated from us in our bedroom by about two inches of plasterboard and wallpaper which line the eaves cupboard. He must have been able to hear us talking.

Squeaker was the first of the gang to pair up. All that extra food and vitamins, I expect. It was, after all, only January. A few days later I managed a closer look at Partlet (wife) and to my delight I noticed the tell-tale yellow by her beak. It was the little one who had been born about two weeks before Squeaker and who had been friendly with him all along. The one I once nearly mistook for Squeaker when Squeaker was lost after his first night out. The one I used to call the juvenile. The one who carried him to the rhododendrons on an early wavering flight, the one who flew to be near him when he was launched from the bedroom window. I felt as if we were taking part in some slushy hearts and flowers romantic novel. I could not have chosen him a better mate myself.

Yveline donated Minou's soft Persian fur combings which I scattered enticingly on the wisteria twigs and I went over the fields and fetched sheep's wool from the barbed wire.

There were some warm days at the start of February. Squeaker spent a great deal of time shouting outside his home. I saw new black feathers on his breast and his cheeks and collar were becoming whiter.

I have to pass under this area when I go to the greenhouse. Squeaker does not like me to go into the greenhouse. Was it because I put him in there on two occasions before he could fly and I had to go out to the shops? He winkles me out from my engrossing tasks therein by flying onto the ridge and running up and down calling. When this fails to elicit me, he pretends to fall and slithers and scrabbles on the sloping glass. That brings me out, of course, and then he has a short chat and flies back up to the roof or leads me to the back door.

On February 11th the snow and cold returned and Squeaker spent a long time over his meals in the utility room, not at all keen to return to his wife. However, once as I watched from my bedroom window, I saw Squeaker give Partlet a tuft of Minou's fur and as soon as she turned her back on him to squeeze under the tiles to put it in place, my devious protégé mounted her.

Two days later Squeaker took up noisy residence in the robins' nest box on the crab apple tree immediately opposite the back door. He called and chirruped loudly and triumphantly from dawn to dusk and only quietened when I approached to remonstrate with him, 'What about Wifey? Your Partlet? The cats can get at this nest. They had the robins last year, you know.'

Undeterred he continued to entice and invite me in. For that was his purpose, I quite soon deduced.

Mother, sensible as usual, had the answer.

'You must take the box down.'

That night after dark, I crept out like a thief and prized the box off the trunk with a jemmy.

He found the great tits' box next and as the hole was too small for him, he perched on a twig beside it, trilling loudly but rather musically for a sparrow, as soon as he saw me emerge from the house. I brought Yveline round to witness his strange behaviour and her comment with full French flavour was:

'Bizarre!'

Yveline is convinced that Squeaker has a fuller and more musical voice than other sparrows, but I suspect she is prejudiced like me.

When I dismantled the great tits' box, there were very few traces left of the bumble bees' nest which I had so rudely disturbed last summer.

The cold miserable March and April thankfully retarded Squeaker's precocious behaviour and he returned to his faithful Partlet.

At the end of April, after much stretching of wings, in her gilded cage, our youngest daughter, Gemma, finally flew the nest. Her independence was overdue but we are bereft.

Squeaker called imperiously from the back door and I hastened with millet to admire his strong masculine appearance. Surely his feathers were glossier than those of the rest of the gang?

22

Family Life

In May Squeaker and Partlet were joined by another, older, pair. Now, in June, the young have hatched and the two males sit under my window sunning themselves whilst the poor little females rush to and fro with aphids and caterpillars. This May the gardens and woods are adrip with green goodies, but I put out soft white bread for Partlet all the same. If I find a froghopper, I extract it and set it on the bird table too, for old times' sake.

One day as Harry and I were resting from our labours in the garden and sipping coffee at a table on the lawn, Squeaker came and busied himself in a dust bath in the flowerbed beside us. We looked down at him indulgently, as he rooted up a rare geranium with his energetic activities, pleased he liked our company. But the next day I filled in the hole and watered the precious plant back in. The sand tray is brought out each dry morning now and is much appreciated – by all of us.

The year has now turned full circle and we rejoice that that once helpless blind blob, which later fought so hard for life despite my bumbling ministrations, lives to take his natural place in the scheme of things.

Our daily charge of emotion, when this free wild bird with a family of its own, swoops down onto head or hand, is echoed by the nineteenth-century American nature writer Henry David Thoreau. He said: 'I once had a sparrow alight on my shoulder for a moment while I was hoeing in a village garden, and I felt that I was more distinguished by that circumstance than I should have been by any epaulet I could have worn.'

In the beginning I know Squeaker could not have survived without me, but now, I wonder, can I do without that bird?

Oakridge, July 1985

Epilogue

On that first day in June 1984 when Squeaker had descended upon us so abruptly, I had assumed that I would just be fostering a small strange creature for three or four weeks at the most. It would grow feathers, open its eyes, learn to feed itself and fly off into the blue and that would be that. More likely it would die before then, however, as at that stage I had never heard of anyone who had managed to raise so young a bird.

I did not take into account the fact that such small creatures have distinct and individual characters. Nor did I expect to fall in love as I did – before the first hour was up.

Nevertheless, I knew that in no way would I attempt to keep Squeaker as a domesticated pet should he survive. Difficult as it made my task when he was rendered flightless by his illness, I could not even contemplate caging him. I think there is something vaguely distasteful about a wild animal or bird made to think that it is anything other than wild and free. I did not want his necessary dependence upon us whilst he was ill to prejudice his chances in the wild.

When, in the autumn of 1984, it was clear he was independent and perfectly integrated with the gang, we left the choice of company to him. We were enormously flattered that he decided he wanted to keep an eye on us as much as we did on him. It became quite routine that each day we would seek each other out. I did not feel guilty about this as I am fairly sure that it was not entirely the food that motivated his actions. For example, sometimes he would just call down at me as I passed under his nest or perch on the gutter, or call to us if we were in the garden as he passed by on his own business. We knew very well his different calls and behaviour when he fancied tit-bits.

Harry usually had the first contact of the day, as he was always up early and the first thing he did was to open the back door with a handful of crumbs and call for Squeaker. Bimbo moaned in protest at having to share our attentions. I'm sure she hated that bird.

We found we talked about Squeaker to each other every day. Just as much as we discussed our children. And in much the same vein: how clever/pretty/delightful/naughty but utterly superior and unique he was. Typically, as the weary commuter returned in the evening, he would brush past me to get to the back garden and call, 'Come along, my bird!'

I, hovering with the sherry, knew I was not the object of his eager eyes.

In July 1985, Viv the bird-seed buyer telephoned. 'I have two baby swifts whose nest has been destroyed. My hands are full with parakeets. One swift is nearly dead and probably won't last the night and I haven't the time to look after them. I think they will both die.'

She knew I would be a sucker when confronted by the moribund orphans. Fortunately the swifts turned out to be house martins. I was relieved because swifts depart for Africa in August and the nestlings would not be mature enough for that. House martins leave in late September or October. Unlike Squeaker and E.T. I could not bring them up and teach them to fly outside as I could not expect or rely on them to return to me.

They had to be kept indoors until they were able to look after themselves, and luckily house martins are smaller than swifts.

This was a challenge. House martins are a very different kettle of crumbs from house sparrows. I had been told very firmly that the former require *live, flying* insects. I rushed to the woods to see what was on the wing. Nothing. I even looked for the poor froghoppers but there were none to be seen. Had I really so depleted them last year that I had altered the whole ecology of the wood? This was another summer of fresh green foliage, untouched by 'dingly-danglies', although in May when Squeaker became a father I seem to recall caterpillars on the crawl. The weather was some of the worst on record. No hot, heavy, fly-swotty days. The practicalities soon forced me to modify 'live, flying' to mean 'fresh insects'.

In normal summer weather, midges and mosquitoes in July make that month quite unpleasant for humans. This year, again, there was a dearth. Have you ever wondered just how many little nipping flying transparencies when mashed up fill half a teacup? As they were so rare this year, and the odd one squashed between finger and thumb leaves hardly a trace, I soon abandoned that source of nourishment for my birds.

Hunting became very time consuming. You know how long it takes to stalk, with rolled newspaper, the *one* buzzing housefly which disturbs your rest. Also, at first, houseflies seemed overly large and crunchy for my small, shocked and delicate foster babies.

During the seven weeks that I was to be their prisoner, I lost a great deal of weight, ran up a huge telephone bill and had to cancel most of my daily social activities.

Mother said, 'It's all because of that sparrow. You mustn't keep telling people about it or you will find you will be tied up every year.'

Secretly I was delighted with my new charges. Squeaker had given me confidence and was a part of our life now. These little waifs had to be prepared for their long journey. I was dedicated but not devoted. Squeaker was exceptional. These birds I would do my duty by. Indeed, it would be very easy as they were far more attractive then baby sparrows. Quieter, more friendly and trusting and nicer natured to each other. They never squabbled with each other as Squeaker and E.T. did. Before they could fly they followed my every move with their eyes. They liked to be held near my face when they would stare trustingly at me.

I promised aloud to them, 'I'll get you to Africa even if it takes all my pocket money and means badgering the airlines.'

The smallest, Baby, was almost dead when he arrived and I had to force feed him every half hour. This entailed prising open the beak with a fingernail, wedging it open and pushing down liquid goodies (pulverized steak, liver and cod liver oil) with the aid of a blunt cocktail stick. As he revived, Baby was found to be very nervous and active. He had dull-brown feathers and bulging eyes in a little skull-like head. He had a very bright and quick intelligence, though, and as soon as he was eating normally his superior intellect manifested itself in countless ways. He was the first to experiment and, although by far the weaker and smaller of the two birds, the first to launch off on flying forays. Thicky, on the other hand, was large, bright blue and white, glossy, placid and untroubled. They were devoted to each other.

Each day I made expeditions to neighbours' houses with my jam jar where I rid every window and greenhouse of all insect life. Every loose paving stone on every patio was raised in search of winged ants and eggs. The small moths in the woods, having laid their eggs, were coming to the end of their life cycle, and, being moribund, were easy to catch. The liver and steak were my mainstay in emergencies. They did actually prefer the steak to any other food, but I persisted with the small insects as they were unlikely to encounter well hung, flying beefsteak in the wild.

I was unable to leave the birds for more than one hour at a time for the whole of their stay with me. I imagine that in the wild when the weather is inclement and insects are unavailable, these birds can fast for quite long periods. However, I wanted to give Thicky and Baby every chance to catch up with their peers.

For a short time, before they could fly, I was able to take them to meetings or luncheons with me. But I would be preoccupied, with darting eyes assessing the insect potential of any buildings or messuage I was currently visiting. Before leaving I would flit round with ambidextrous hands snapping and swatting to fill the empty matchbox which had now become a permanent accessory in my handbag.

The first feed of the day was any time from 5 a.m. As soon as I heard their enquiring little twitters, I would scoop them out of their nest (dismantled feather duster and tissues in an ice cream carton) and sit them on my chest as I stayed in bed and aimed pre-prepared food down their throats. Then we all three dozed under the duvet and when they wanted more food they cheeped and crawled up to my face on their short hairy legs. Yes, little pink legs covered in white hairs!

As with all nestlings they were easy to house train but it was a different matter when they learned to fly. A house martin's nest usually first attracts one's attention by the thick spatter of droppings all over the wall and ground below it. They learned to fly in our newly decorated bedroom which was the safest place to keep them. It has large windows on three sides and I placed their nest (now a feather-lined tea box, more like the real thing) on top of a wardrobe facing our bed. It was as near as possible the same height from the ground as their nest outside would have been. Unfortunately, the new wallpaper, curtains and pelmets were in the palest of off-whites. Every day I renewed the newspaper covering bed, tables, wardrobes, curtains, TV, telephone and all the carpet. There were many roosting places, favourites being picture frames and wall lights.

As their flying skills improved, they delighted us with their perpetual figures-of-eight around the room. The windows were kept closed as, although they could fly quite well, they were quite unable to feed themselves. I wanted to fatten them up for their long migration in a few short weeks. Baby was still very tiny but much noisier and more active than Thicky.

I tried to train them to take living insects by impaling a fly or moth on a cocktail stick and passing it in front of their faces. Baby soon cottoned on. Thicky tried and tried but invariably missed and watched in what appeared to be admiration as Baby dextrously snatched the prey.

We enjoyed our living mobiles but knew they had to be made independent to get to Africa. On August 6th I opened the bedroom window. Thicky did his usual figure-of-eight and then overshot straight out of the window and was lost to sight in seconds. Baby pulled up short and avoided the open window all day.

It was tragic. He looked all over the bedroom for his brother, in and under favourite perches. He pined and pined. He never made another tweet or cheep from that day nor did he ever go back into their nest. He now spent the nights on the bracket of the wall light over our heads when we were lying in bed. I had to rig up a platform to catch his droppings.

I was still worried about his health and size and gave daily doses of vitamins. He relied on me for company more and more. It was a nasty dilemma. If I let him go too soon he would surely die as the weather had turned so bad, and if he stayed much longer he would become too imprinted on me to survive in the wild. Eventually I resolved that the first sunny day that insects were on the wing, he would have to go.

On August 28th I said, 'Bon voyage,' to my little friend as he wheeled over the roof and was lost to sight. I sadly rolled up the newspapers for the last time, aware that we would never know what happened to our protégés.

Often, during the winter of 1985/6 as I watched Squeaker and Partlet, I was reminded of those other two birds, and wondered if they had made it to warmer climes. It was a difficult winter for our family and a nasty winter weatherwise. Many a choice plant was killed in the garden but Squeaker and Partlet flourished. In the spring they started to refurbish their nest under the roof tiles beneath our bedroom window, but the older pair did not join them.

This year one of the old males of the gang died. He spent the last two weeks of his life amongst my potted plants in the utility room. I used to leave the door slightly ajar for Squeaker to pop in and out and this old bird took advantage to creep in unnoticed each morning. He was almost blind and could hardly fly but always managed to get outside to roost before dusk. Whenever I appeared he clumsily scrabbled and scrambled to hide behind leaves, so I tactfully pretended not to notice him and left millet, as if by accident, in a nearby potted plant.

It is possibly an unusual thing for a wild bird to choose to spend its last days in such unaccustomed closeness to humans and we were flattered by his trust.

On Sunday May 4th I watched proudly as Squeaker and Partlet copulated with uninhibited zest on the gutter outside their nest. Last year two youngsters had been raised by the gang but I could not be sure of their parentage as Squeaker and Partlet had been sharing the same covered nesting area with the older pair. However, I am fairly sure Squeaker's parents were still feeding the magpies and crows with *their* newly hatched offspring every few weeks. On several occasions I had heard raucous noises of large birds fighting over goodies on the terrace before I was up and once I found the remains of a pecked chick. The parents never seemed to be feeding young and I never heard the nestlings cheeping for more than a day. It always made me think that that would have been Squeaker's fate had Gemma not been at that spot on that day.

Would it have been better? When Squeaker was so ill and becoming psychologically disturbed with instinct and learning at war in his little crippled, flightless body, I felt that I was being rapped over the knuckles by Dame Nature in no uncertain way.

But that determined, brave and intelligent creature taught us things about ourselves and each other as well as birds. Indeed, all seemed vindicated when he emerged from his unusual babyhood and youth into a fine example of his species, leading a normal healthy life. He even had a slight advantage. Being an opportunist, like all his kind, he exploited our slavish devotion (manifested by the production of endless supplies of millet, peeled sunflower seeds, vitamins, etc.) and was able to use spare food-hunting time to play in his sandpit, sit around with Partlet, sunbathe on the roof or call us from the house. We even watched fairly indulgently as he ignored our shouting and delicately decapitated our crocuses, staring at us with a defiant beady black eye. (Perhaps the flowers contained some substance needed in his diet, we reasoned. The others could jolly well keep off though.)

It had been such a dismal spring that we were particularly looking forward to the warmer summer weather when we would be out in the garden and our little friend would join us, perching in a nearby bush or flowerbed for little quiet chats in a sub-song meant only for our ears. And occasionally I would encourage him back onto my finger. The future seemed assured as I watched with smug pride the activities of our foster bird and his mate. But that sunny Sunday May 4th turned out to be the last time we ever saw Squeaker. We are bereft.

Partlet stayed on the nest and used to emerge when I called 'Squeaker!' She flew down when I offered food but was too shy to come near until I went back into the house.

Fifteen days after Squeaker's disappearance and almost certain demise (cat? car?), Partlet plucked up courage to do something she had never done before, which was to enter the house. I have been reluctant to use words such as 'courage' and 'bravery' as characteristics of creatures other than human, as we have been told that other animals are not capable of logical thought processes and all their actions are triggered off by

97

pre-programmed instinctive reflex behaviour connected with preservation of the species. This is probably true for the most part, but I cannot think of any other way to describe certain activities displayed by Squeaker. For example, when he was flightless and his toes curled under his feet, he would have been quite happy to sit down all day, but to please me and for no food reward, he struggled to co-operate with the rather painful physiotherapy I devised. I am sure the apparent altruism displayed by the three unrelated sparrows who lifted Squeaker to safety when he was learning to fly was purely an instinctive reaction to save the species. One could argue, of course, that it is the very same instinctive reaction which motivates a non-swimming stranger to dive into deep water to attempt to rescue a drowning child and that a posthumous medal is inappropriate for such behaviour.

Throughout this story I have tried not to be anthropomorphic as I am very well aware how the amateur and sometimes professional naturalist can misconstrue the actions and express-ions of animals. I didn't quite succeed. But surely tales of animals warning owners of fire, fetching help to the injured, finding and warming frozen bodies and dolphins saving drowning sailors cannot all be apocryphal?

With regard to the following episode, I fortunately had a witness and a camera to hand and I leave the readers to draw their own conclusions.

Partlet flew into the utility room, up its whole length and turned left through the doorway into the kitchen. Even Squeak-er had not done that since he had grown up. Despite the presence of two humans (one a total stranger and, as luck would have it, a bird phobic) and the dog, she slowly and methodically searched behind every heating pipe, cluttered shelf, storage jar and picture frame. Even the click of the camera, controlled terror of my guest and deep growling, longing-to-pounce scrab-blings of Bimbo as I clung onto her collar failed to panic the bird from her task. When she had quite finished, she flew to the top of the door, had a final look round, then flew back the way she had come.

If my conclusions drawn from that activity are anywhere near correct, Partlet would have had to delve deep into her memory for things she had witnessed as a young bird many months ago and never since, she would have had to make deductions from those memories and, against all her instinct of self-preservation, behave in a way that in normal circumstances would have been anathema to her. In other words she put two and two together. That she made five was not through lack of logic and I cried for her.

In due course the eggs hatched and I made sure that Partlet had plenty of moist brown bread to help out with feeding her family. Squeaker's offspring.

After a while another youngish male joined Partlet and he appeared to be a most diligent step-father taking in food to the nest. We are most pleased – for all their sakes.

There are five juvenile sparrows in our garden this year. Three are Squeaker's progeny and two, about a week younger, from another pair. They form a noisy new gang. We refer to them as 'the yellow beak squadron'.

They have some curious habits, the most noticeable being that as no adults were feeding them after they came out of their nests, they stick together and feed each other. Partlet and her new mate are very busy courting and refurbishing the nest and there is no sign of the parents of the younger pair.

The yellow beak squadron sometimes perch in a row like baby blue tits on a swaying twig and *scream* for attention at my back door. No diffident cheeps or even loud chirrups, but a shrieking, demanding chorus. Of course I run with soaked dog biscuits and wet bread. Bimbo fumes.

They also post a look-out at the front of the house on a bush directly opposite the kitchen window. When I put the crumbs out, the rest of the squad materializes. One I call the Beggar immediately goes into action, crouching, fluttering its wings and cheeping like a baby. The others always feed it, sometimes leaving nothing for themselves. When their backs are turned I have noticed that it is quite capable of pecking up food for itself. Sometimes, before it can get going with its act, one of the others snatches a crumb and flies off. The rest of the gang ignore the selfsame food at their feet and fly off in hot pursuit. Occasionally they are all begging from each other and the food is ignored until they sort out who will be 'mum'.

The only adult who ever joins in their food forays is a male bird about three years old. He suddenly turned up one day and seems to be a loner. When I first spotted him, I took an eager look at his left foot, but the little toe was as straight as the others and I chided myself for harbouring false hopes.

Oakridge, July 1987

1 and **2** Male house sparrows in winter (*above*) and spring (*below*).
Notice the less extensive black bib on the lower bird – an individual
variation – but the dark bill of the breeding season male indicates that
he is in breeding condition.

Top **3** A typical perch for a male house sparrow advertising a nest under the gutter.
Bottom **4** Male house sparrow at the entrance of a 'free-standing' nest.

Top **5** The female feeding well grown chick in a house martin's nest which the house sparrows have taken over.
Bottom **6** The cock feeding a chick at the entrance of a well made and recently erected nest-box.

7 and 8 Male and female
at the entrance to a
typical nest site
in weatherboarding
of an old building.

Top **9** Copulation generally takes place right by the nest site and the two males in the background will probably interfere with this attempt at the bathing pool.
Bottom **10** A male house sparrow bringing good-sized green wigwogs (in this case insect larvae) for its chicks.

Top **11** A white-headed variant of adult female house sparrow – in some areas many of the birds have some white in their plumage. *Bottom* **12** This male has an overgrown upper mandible possibly caused through breaking the tip of the lower one by flying into a window. The bird is well able to feed itself but its plumage is rather scruffy as it has difficulty preening.

13 Three house sparrows crowd onto the hand of a regular bird feeder in St James's Park.

14 In some areas the house sparrows have learnt to hover beside nut feeders – in this case the bird can just reach it from a nearby perch.

Top **15** Wheatsheafs are not a common sight in the modern
countryside but a hungry sparrow would hardly know where to start!
Bottom **16** On the other hand millions of our modern house sparrows
still rely on the wheat, processed into bread, for their daily food.

SPARROWS IN THE WILD

Sparrows in the Wild

When she was chosen by Squeaker, Loraine started to build up a relationship with one of the most widespread and familiar species of birds in the world. House sparrows, whether occurring naturally or as an introduced species, are a part of the everyday life of millions of people and, as such common and humdrum companions, tend to be ignored by almost everyone. Birdwatchers often look down their noses, rather than through their binoculars, at a bird that is neither a rarity from far away nor an inhabitant of a romantic wilderness area. As Loraine has discovered, one does miss a great deal by not taking sparrowdom seriously.

In fact there are scientists who live and breathe sparrow for, as one might expect of a group of birds that live so successfully with man, too many sparrows can be a real menace to some human enterprises. Large flocks of sparrows can eat a great deal of food and reduce the yield of standing crops. The birds can ravage and contaminate stored grain, they can spread infection in kitchens and factories and even despoil the gardener's favourite flowers.

However, they also provide a great deal of enjoyment for their human friends and they have the great advantage, over the rarer species of bird, in that they are always around to be watched. Loraine was in the very privileged position of being able to observe many of the minutiae of sparrow life which ordinary watchers would find very difficult – if not impossible.

For example the extraordinary indoor search by Partlet in the utility room and kitchen, for the missing Squeaker, completely out of character but showing a very detailed memory of events which happened many months ago, could not possibly have been observed in a completely wild population.

However, I do not believe that we should be too surprised by such examples of long-term memory in any bird: this is exactly the sort of knowledge that may be needed for a bird to survive well. The memories of where a good meal was found last year or of how a predator was avoided will have very obvious survival benefits.

There is only one previous observation which in any way can be said to parallel Partlet's search. This was by Summers-Smith, in his monograph on the species, *The House Sparrow* (Collins New Naturalist Monograph 19, 1963), which reports the amazing actions of a pair of house sparrows that built their nest in a cavity wall behind a rusted-through ventilation grille. When this hole in the grille was closed, because the office workers indoors were being disturbed by the calls of the young, the parent birds flew indoors through an open window and made their way into the closed side of the nest through the inner (again rusted) grille. So far as was known neither of the parent birds had ever ventured inside the building before. Thus the birds were not only being very brave going in through the window but they were also showing a good sense of deduction.

For only one of Loraine's observations am I unable to find a parallel in the literature or an explanation in modern behavioural thinking – which has been able to explain so much animal behaviour in terms of a survival advantage to the individual (or at least to a close relative bearing some of its own genes): that is in the observation of the other, unrelated, sparrows helping youngsters with their first flights by supporting them from below. Loraine has seen this several times but, of course, each incident has only lasted for moments. However, in the wild, most youngsters are capable of good, strong flight before they leave the nest and so it may be that they seldom have to help weak and wobbly youngsters, which may elicit a different response from the normal. It is true that there are some records of very small chicks being transferred from one nest to another by their parents, most often when the original nest has been disturbed. This could be an explanation for the fairly frequent appearance of the nestlings thrown out or dropped from nests. However, such very young chicks clearly would have no chance of transfer, from nest to nest, on their parent's backs, and it seems most likely that they would be carried in the beak.

To start with I shall try to summarize what is known of the house sparrow as it lives naturally, as compared with the rather artificial early months of Squeaker's life. Then I will describe the life of the bird through its year; of course even Squeaker had real sparrow parents and so the year begins with the breeding attempts of the adult birds and not with the hatching of the rather hideous chick from the egg. Because of the very sensible way that Squeaker was brought up, with maximum liberty at all times, much of his life was quite natural.

What is a House Sparrow?

To a scientist each house sparrow is a member of the species *Passer domesticus*. There are about twenty other species in the genus *Passer* and all occur naturally in the Old World. These sparrows are quite closely related to the rock sparrows and snowfinches and are rather more distantly related to the hundreds of species of finches and buntings. The American sparrows are not particularly closely akin to ours – they are more like buntings. *Passer* sparrows are quite small birds with strong beaks designed for seed-eating. Most of them live in close proximity to man.

All the species are mainly brown and grey in plumage. In Britain there are two species – the house sparrow and the tree sparrow. Tree sparrows, *Passer montanus*, are much more rural birds than house sparrows; the sexes are alike and the birds look superficially like adult male house sparrows.

However, they have bright chocolate-brown crowns and are a

105

little smaller than the house sparrow. Tree sparrows seem to be subject to wide fluctuations in population levels in Britain and from a recent peak at the end of the 1960s have declined considerably so that they are now rarely seen over most of Scotland, Wales and Ireland and have declined in many parts of England. They are easily overlooked but their sharp *chip* call, often given in flight, is a giveaway to clued-up birdwatchers.

The appearance of young house sparrows of both sexes and of females of all ages is very similar, which is why Loraine could not know that Squeaker was going to be a male or what E.T. would turn out to be. They lack the black bib and grey-centred chestnut head of the males – who acquire their distinctive plumage during the moult in the autumn after they hatch. When they are in breeding condition males also have black bills rather than the horn colour outside the breeding season. House sparrows quite often have a white feather or two in their plumage. This is a partial albinism and is usually the result of a genetic defect, although sometimes caused by trauma; full albinos, with all-white plumage and pink eyes, are very unlikely to survive in the wild. Quite often the amount of albinism shown increases with age in the same individual and some rather pretty piebald birds may result. Their strange coloration does not seem to put off their mates and they are capable of breeding successfully – and passing on the albinistic genes to future generations.

What about the sparrow's relatively modest vocal prowess? After all Loraine named Squeaker after the first insistent sounds that a baby sparrow makes to show it needs food. These noises, as Loraine records, are used by the youngster through the whole of its time in the nest and also after it has fledged, whilst it is dependent on the parents to feed it. Some people believe that these calls are not only to alert the parents to the chick's hunger but are also used as a dangerous kind of double bluff – if you do not feed me, the noise I am making will attract a predator and I will be killed and so your genes will not be carried on to the next generation.

106

The loud *cheep* or double syllable *chit-ip* notes are most obvious from the males during the spring and summer but they can be heard at any time of the year. This is the origin of the French name for the sparrow – 'chipeau' and 'sparrow' itself has probably developed from an ancient onomatopoeic name. This call sometimes develops into a staccato rattle at times of excitement – as during the communal chases. There are also softer calls used in flight, and on the ground, for contact between members of the same flock. The chats that Squeaker and Loraine engaged in were probably of this nature. No one normally pays much attention to these chirps and cheeps although, when advertising his potential nest site just above one's bedroom window, it is sometimes very difficult to ignore the almost rhythmic and very insistent stream of calls from a resident male. However, this primitive repertoire of sounds and a fairly simple series of behaviour patterns have enabled the humdrum house sparrow to become one of the world's most successful species of bird.

The Extent of Sparrowdom

There are few areas in Britain and Ireland where man lives that do not have their own breeding populations of house sparrows. Over the last 150 years the species has spread to the northernmost parts of the country and even to the offshore islands. This has partly been due to the spread of cereal-growing northwards as the human population has increased and as new methods of husbandry have been introduced. In a few instances house sparrows have retreated from the remotest areas as farming regimes have altered. For instance in some highland areas in Wales, the Pennines and Scotland the house sparrow populations round farms have gone with the demise of the horse as the main source of mobile power – dropped oats are a palatable food but no house sparrow has yet been able to sustain itself on spilt diesel!

Indeed, the whole economy of the house sparrow within urban Britain must have undergone a huge and largely un-documented change over the last eighty years or so. The number of horses in cities at the turn of the century and the amount of food available scattered by the horses, available from their bedding and even passing through them must have been phenomenal. The human population would have been much lower and therefore built-up areas much less extensive, but it seems likely that the density of house sparrows would have been much higher. On the other hand, the habit of feeding birds in gardens and parks was not nearly as widespread and it is quite likely that this will have more than compensated for the loss of horse-associated feeding possibilities.

The provision of food for garden poultry, particularly during the last war, probably made a great difference to house sparrows. It was at about that time that the use of the birds as food by country people became a thing of the past; within living memory, there used to be many areas where large fowling nets were used to catch roosting sparrows for the pot during the winter. Indeed, until midway through the last century, nesting house sparrows were sometimes attracted to breed in specially constructed earthenware pots – whose design can be traced back to Roman times – from which the youngsters were easily taken to be eaten.

This exploitation of the house sparrow for food went hand in hand with steady efforts to rid the countryside and the crops of the attention of the birds. Children were employed to scare the birds from the crops and many parish registers record the payment of bounties for killing them. These ranged from two or three pence per dozen in the eighteenth century to a shilling a dozen a hundred years ago. From some parish records it seems that more than 20,000 house sparrows may have been killed locally in a single year. Even from these records it can be seen that the principles of ecological management were beginning to be understood – in some parishes lesser amounts of money were made available for young birds and for eggs. Indeed, there are records in some archives which show that a premium was placed on adult birds killed at the beginning of the breeding season.

How many house sparrows are there in Britain? Not a question with a simple and exact answer, for the sad fact is that, for any species of small birds, there is a lot of death about and so, outside the breeding season, the population is always falling. This is quite a natural situation, for a stable population only requires each pair of adults to rear a couple of youngsters that survive to replace them in the breeding population. With an average of two breeding attempts each season and four eggs laid each time there are, potentially, ten birds at the end of the season for every pair that started. If one could wave a magic wand and allow all these to survive to the next season and then breed – and so on – for only five years, a single pair at the start would still be alive and have 6,248 offspring alive.

So these deaths are a necessary factor that allows a balance in nature. They happen at all stages from the egg onwards. Detailed studies of wild breeding birds show that desertions and infertility account for almost 29% of the eggs laid. Of the chicks that hatch some 74% fledge, and so the overall breeding success is just a little better than an average of one youngster for every two eggs laid. Loraine's success with Squeaker but failure with E.T. shows that she and Yveline were about as good at the job as a pair of house sparrows.

These figures seem to indicate that, for every pair of adults, there should be four extra youngsters about at the end of the breeding season. Unfortunately death raises its ugly head again for there are significant losses both to the adults and to the youngsters during the course of the breeding season. Breeding attempts are interrupted and whole clutches and broods may be lost. At one nest site intensively studied by Denis Summers-Smith from the start of one summer to the end of the fifth four different males and three different females were involved. During three of the summers two broods were reared but only one in each of the other two. The young birds, freshly out of the nest, are very vulnerable to all sorts of hazards from drowning in ponds, getting waterlogged in bad weather, meeting cars on roads, cats in gardens and crashing into windows whilst in flight. It is quite likely that more than half the fledglings die within a month of leaving the nest.

The population calculations that have been made show that, from its low point at the start of the breeding season, the population almost doubles by the end of July or beginning of August. At this stage the youngsters outnumber the adults by about four to three. They are still more likely to die than their parents and by the start of winter the age ratio is about evens and, when the breeding season starts again, there are about four birds reared the previous year for every five adults. If we think in terms of 'expectation of further life', the youngster about four weeks out of the nest will last, on average, a further seven or eight months. That means the 'average' fledgling probably cannot expect to have a chance of breeding at all. However if it survives to celebrate its first New Year's Day it has an average expectation of further life of about twenty months.

So what does this mean in terms of numbers? The best guess is that there are about 5 million pairs of house sparrows in Britain at the start of the breeding season so that the population peaks during the summer at about 20 million birds. Because of the mortality during the early part of the breeding season there are actually about this number (20 million) of sparrow deaths each year.

One might think, with all this death, that the streets of every town and village would be knee deep in pathetic sparrow corpses throughout the year but, of course, for many creatures a dead sparrow is a tasty meal. The birds that die will be eaten by scavengers like foxes, magpies, rooks and crows (particularly eating them off the roads). Others will quickly be disposed of by insects – flies will lay their eggs on the corpse and the maggots disintegrate them over a period of a few days, while sexton beetles will actually bury the corpse as a source of food for their grubs.

Many sparrows are actually killed for food not just by cats but also by kestrels, sparrowhawks and tawny owls. Individuals of all three of these avian predators may specialize in catching house sparrows and to them the sparrow is a very important part of their diet. In the case of some of the urban kestrels and tawny owls this may be true throughout the year. In the territory of such predators they may well be the most important cause of death – otherwise it is very difficult to quantify the risk from particular sources.

The recovery details of ringed birds will, of course, give a biased sample. Biased, that is, towards causes of death likely to be reported by the finders and likely to result in the corpse coming to someone's attention. Being caught by Tibbles and brought, triumphantly, into the kitchen is a good way of getting your ring reported – being taken ill and dying in the thick ivy on a church wall is not a good way of becoming a statistic at the British Trust for Ornithology. Of the 'recoveries' (that is, of dead sparrows) reported most are just 'found' but the following categories appear amongst 3,414 recoveries reported so far:

Reported cause of death	Percentage
Cats	19.1
Traffic	9.5
Inside something	4.5
Shot or trapped	3.4
Predators (not cats)	2.0
Accidentally by man	1.3
Collisions (windows or wires)	1.1
Unspecified	59.1

These statistics conceal all sorts of bizarre and unfortunate accidents but the main categories are fairly self-explanatory.

'Traffic' includes birds found dead on the road and so a few which flew into roadside wires will also appear here. Birds inside things are mostly trapped in buildings – often during the breeding season when they are prospecting for nesting sites. 'Shot or trapped' includes birds vandalized by small boys with air rifles and also those destroyed as agricultural pests. 'Accidentally taken by man' includes some birds in rat and mouse traps, those dying from eating poison put out for other species, caught in fruit netting or even trapped in cotton to keep them off the spring crocus flowers.

A handful of deaths are caused by man in very unusual circumstances. For instance flying sparrows have sometimes met a golf ball and their end at the same time; there is a stuffed house sparrow in the Long Room at Lords, which was a young-ster killed by a ball bowled in the Cambridge University v. MCC match of 1936. Nothing could, of course, be worse for the individual sparrow; rather more serious for man is the damage done to jet engines by birds sucked into them – with other species this has caused large-scale loss of human life. For many years the areas of runways at airports have been carefully managed to make sure that they are not attractive to any species of birds but sparrows have been known to meet their end in this very high-tech fashion.

With modern burglar alarms, set to react to any movement or even to the body heat of an intruder, sparrows inside buildings can nowadays cause mayhem. This is especially the case with computer-controlled systems that are programmed to come on at a particular time and cannot be manually reset. I am not sure what a frantic office manager can do as the witching hour approaches and the darned sparrow continues to fly round the bank building. The practical solution of shooting the bird does seem a bit drastic and may lead to extensive and expensive redecoration. All bird ringers realize that they are amongst the most difficult of all birds to catch – particularly if you want one individual.

Quite apart from the birds themselves, their nests can be a real source of embarrassment. Many people become very annoyed by their habit of usurping the beautifully constructed mud nests which house martins build under eaves. The sparrows may take them over whilst the house martins are still building or chip their way into the finished nests over the winter – whilst the rightful owners are away in Africa. Even the most pro-sparrow people try to prevent this from happening as they feel that natural justice should decree that the martins are able to use the nests they have built. Humans can tip the balance in their favour in a variety of different ways. Artificial house martin nests can be put up – they are made from material too hard for the sparrows to chip the necessary few millimetres from the lip. Or, if the house martins leave in the autumn with their nests in good condition, a stiff wash of cement over the mud may armour them against the sparrows. The other measure to take is to hang some heavy metal nuts or other weights on strings about six inches long in front of the nests – the house martins arrive with a curving upwards swoop and miss the strings but the sparrows come in horizontally and cannot make it so easily.

House martins are not the only species to be thrown out. Swift sites in roof spaces can be taken over by house sparrows in the spring, long before their migrant owners return. In sand martin colonies the burrows may be taken over by sparrows but, in this case, no harm is generally done, for the sand martins will easily be able to dig new tunnels. Garden nestboxes, with entrances of more than 1.25" diameter, may be taken over by house sparrows – keep the hole size smaller than this to exclude them and only allow in the tits. As you will remember, Squeaker even tried to get Loraine into a nesting box. In some areas the sparrows strike up a relationship with rooks, even herons, and build their own nests within the foundation of the larger species' more massive structures.

It is when the house sparrow starts to build in ventilation

ducts, electrical equipment, lorry engines, elevator mechanisms and even within the control channels in aircraft wings that real damage can be caused. From the bird's point of view all these sites have really good nesting potential since they are cosy, inaccessible and available. From the architect's or engineer's angle the sparrows are unexpected and highly unwelcome visitors often causing costly modification of design or the erection of unsightly netting or baffles. Even birds building in roof spaces can be a great hazard, for more and more nest material may be brought in each year so that, after a relatively short time in the life of the building, literally tons of highly inflammable material may be piled up.

The house sparrow must be one of the world's most successful and adaptable species, for it has spread over much of North and South America where it was introduced about a century ago. The sparrow's success has come from a very exploitative attitude, on the bird's part, where any possible nook or cranny may be investigated for breeding potential and any source of food is fair game. This has not been accomplished with any loss of guile or wariness on the part of the birds – indeed they remain very much on the alert at all times. Even the birds crowding to be fed, or perching on the tourist's hands, in central London always have an eye open for lurking danger. Of course Squeaker looked upon Loraine and her friends as his parents but seems to have learnt from the other sparrows, when he took his place amongst them, that humankind should not be trusted although throughout his life he was reasonably relaxed in the presence of known humans.

In some parts of the world the tree sparrow takes over from the house sparrow as the bird of urban areas. This is true in the Far East and it is clear from the superb illustrations of both Chinese and Japanese artists that the attitude of the humans to their birds closely mirrors most town dwellers in Britain who, whether they are bird-minded or not, have a sneaking affection for the *Cockney Sparrer*.

The Sparrow Year

A male house sparrow without a nest site will never be able to attract a mate; it is difficult for us as humans to say whether the hen bird picks the male or his real estate in such cases. However, the breeding pair is not, by any means, necessarily two unmated and inexperienced birds coming together to breed. As with Partlet's remating after Squeaker's demise, the pair is very often formed as a direct result of the death of one or other member of an established couple. This may take place very swiftly after the death of the mate and the earlier pair's nest site will, of course, be home for the new birds. Divorce seems to be very unusual among sparrows although it seems very common amongst other species which, unlike the house sparrow, do not have a very strong attachment to the nest site. So few house sparrows live anything like their potential lifespan that there is no question of the pair mating for life or the one who is spared pining away when their spouse dies.

So quickly do sparrows find new mates at good nest sites that canny gunners, when there was a bounty for sparrows, would often shoot one of the pair from local nests and leave the other to attract a replacement mate. They could be sure that a new mate would be in residence within a few days who, in its turn, could be shot. This implies a surplus of un-mated birds in the population or, just possibly, a chronic shortage of good nest sites. However, the answer may not be as simple as that, for all surveys of house sparrows have shown a regular social structure with the nests clumped in particular areas: a colony structure.

These colonies are very obvious when they are confined to farm buildings amidst arable land with no other obvious sites

115

available. In built-up areas, which apparently have huge numbers of suitable sites available, the colonial nature is not nearly
so obvious. However if you count them and plot the nest sites
out it becomes very striking indeed. For example a study in a
rural area in Hampshire showed that the average colony took in
less than half a dozen houses but, throughout the 250 he
surveyed, only about 25% of the buildings had any nests in
them. Another survey, with the houses much closer together,
showed two colonies with nests in 10 out of 12 and 22 out of 27
houses respectively. Between these two colonies was a 'no
sparrow's land' of 15 houses. So in this area about two-thirds of
the houses had house sparrow nests. Loraine's house is
obviously within the territory of a traditional colony. With so
much social interaction going on between the sparrows it is
quite possible that the central breeding sites in a colony are
particularly attractive, and a widow or widower with such a site
– such as Partlet had – would be irresistible to any passing bird
of the opposite sex.

The most likely time for a young cock to set up home, on his
own account, is early in the spring. If he is able to find a suitable
site for a nest, which has not already been claimed by an
established pair, he will spend a great deal of time perched
conspicuously near it chirruping excitedly whenever a female
sparrow approaches. The chirruping will get increasingly insistent and the cock will hop in and out of the nest site – for all the
world like a pushy estate agent desperate for a sale. Often the
female will be uninterested and he may follow her as she goes
away but, if she comes closer and attempts to enter the nest-
hole, aggression on the part of the cock may re-assert itself. This
has to be quickly suppressed or his chance of pairing will be lost.
In Squeaker's case he found a nest site under the gutter below
Loraine's bedroom window during January and paired up with
Partlet, although he had apparently not been displaying a lot,
on January 23rd; which was just after the snow had gone.
Immediately they had paired both started nest building.

According to Loraine, Partlet did not need much wooing as she had attached herself to Squeaker almost as soon as he appeared when launched from the bedroom window as a very young bird. It is very unlikely that this was in any way a sexual attraction, but simply a neighbourly 'get-together' at such an early stage.

However, in many cases the site will already have a nest in it for there will often be few acceptable nesting places within a colony's area which are unoccupied. At a fresh site building will often have been started by the cock bird on his own; he may even have completed the basic structure – a grass or straw ball about the size of a large grapefruit with a single entrance.

Within a large hole much bigger and more untidy structures may be built. In Squeaker's case he may not have built much in the way of a nest when he paired off with Partlet since Loraine had not noticed nest-building activity. Eventually, with the pair working together, the nest will be lined with soft material and usually has a good supply of feathers (over 1,000 have been counted from a single nest). The birds may fight other pairs over these, if they are scarce, and will sometimes travel several hundred metres to a good supply. They have even been seen apparently pecking particularly desirable flank feathers from unsuspecting doves and pigeons.

The male will be helped in the construction of the nest by the female as soon as the pair has been formed and, very often, the few days immediately after she has joined him sees a frenzy of nest-building activity. In extreme cases nests can take only hours to be built and, where one has been destroyed when the female was ready to lay, the egg may be deposited on the construction site. Other nests can be titivated for weeks, even months, during the autumn, winter and early spring before breeding starts. Although the most usual nest sites are in holes, cracks and crevices in buildings or trees, by no means all are. Indeed the domed nature of the nest, unnecessary if it were designed always for a hole, shows that the house sparrow's

ancestors built 'free-standing' homes. These are still fairly frequently found in some areas and whole colonies may be in
hedgerow thorns if there are no suitable buildings in the vicinity. These nests look very untidy and one might expect them to
be more vulnerable to predators, but the birds using them are
often successful. The nests may well need much more care and
attention than enclosed ones but new material can be added to
either type at almost any time of year.

The nest continues to be used, for night-time roosting, during
the winter as protection from the bad weather and is very
important for the adult birds' survival. Some house sparrows,
without suitable breeding sites, will construct roosting 'nests' in
the autumn and use them through the winter. Both members of
established pairs will roost together overnight in the nest. There
is therefore an obvious reason for the vicious fights that sometimes develop against intruders who try to turf out the 'rightful'
occupants of a nest. However since they live in colonies, sparrows may nest very close together – often within less than a
metre if there are two adjacent suitable sites.

For most of the winter time the pair will show little mutual
sexual activity. When the time comes it is the male who initiates
proceedings by drawing himself stiffly upright and hopping,
rather mechanically, towards the female bowing as he
approaches. To start with the female simply turns and flies or
hops away but, as the breeding season approaches, she becomes receptive to these advances and signals her consent by
crouching down with wings part opened and shivering, whilst
quietly cheeping. The male will mount her for a few seconds,
hop off and then generally the whole cycle is repeated again and
again – especially during the week before egg-laying. Up to
twenty or thirty successive copulations may happen in the
space of ten or fifteen minutes. Fertilization takes place when
sperm pass from the cloaca of the male to that of the female; she
twists hers round until it is almost pointing upwards and can
make contact with the male. Copulations usually take place very

close to the nest entrance; with Squeaker and Partlet, often on the gutter immediately above it. This persistent, if uncompli- cated, display of sexual athletics has led to all sorts of popular expressions along the line of 'as randy as a cock sparrer'.

However, life is rarely as simple as this seems. If the female is not receptive and the cock makes advances towards her, she will often attack him and fly off, with him in vociferous pursuit. Almost instantly the other local males will follow the pair and a scrum of 'randy sparrers' will apparently be determined on a gang bang. In such circumstances the female will repel their advances and the whole unsavoury incident, to a human way of looking at it, will be over in 30 seconds to two minutes. In fact it seems that these communal displays have a very important function in stimulating the birds in a colony to come into breeding condition.

Birds, like most wild animals but unlike humans, are not normally in a physiological state to be able to breed: the ovaries of the females and the testes of the males regress during winter to a tiny fraction of their size during the breeding season. The spring-time increase in size is stimulated in various ways. For instance the lengthening spring days register with the bird's hormonal system and may help to start the process. Also, with colonial species, the social interaction between the pairs in the colony helps to bring about the onset of the breeding season and to synchronize it. Individual birds come into breeding condition at different times – one that has suffered injury that prevents it from feeding efficiently may be much later coming into condi- tion.

Synchronization of breeding is quite important. It means that the individual pairs within the colony are likely to be at the same stage in the cycle at the same time. In particular the youngsters are likely to fledge from their nests at the same time and so they will be able to team up with their neighbours' offspring in the post-breeding flock. It also means that the colony breeding date is a compromise between several different pairs; their collective wisdom is much more likely to get the timing right, in relation to the season, than an individual pair's guess. This may have been quite important in the mists of antiquity when the ancestral sparrows were breeding communally so they were able to exploit crops of weed seeds springing up after tropical rains. It is not so important now they are sponging off man (or in this case woman) so successfully.

If all is well the hen will lay the first egg of the pair's first clutch at the end of April or beginning of May. The date will depend on the weather – later in cold springs, earlier in warm ones. It will also depend on the part of the country – much earlier in the south than in the north and also much later in highland areas. In fact the comparison through the species' range – south to north in Europe – is illuminating, since the breeding season starts in mid-March in North Africa and southern Spain but not until mid-May in Scandinavia. Fairly regularly, where there is abundant food available, even British clutches may be started in March. Nesting totally 'out of season' has been reported exceptionally.

The eggs are generally laid in the early morning, one per day, until the clutch is complete. In Britain the average is about 4 eggs per complete clutch – almost exactly this at the start of the season and rising to a peak of 4.3 in June and then declining to 4 again. In Britain well over 90% of clutches have between 3 and 5 eggs with very few records of 7, the maximum recorded from a single hen. In a very few cases two hens have been known to lay in a single nest and 10 or more eggs have resulted. The eggs have a pale ground colour finely spotted in various shades of grey and brown. The overall colour may vary within a clutch but this should not be taken to indicate laying by different females but rather represents the variation in egg pigmentation from the single hen.

It is difficult to say when incubation proper starts but, even during the laying period, one or other of the parents is quite likely to be in residence during daylight. The hen generally roosts in the nest at night and the male may join her. Incubation – that is the keeping of the eggs warm by physical contact with the parent – will definitely have started by the time the third egg has been laid. From then on a parent will be on the nest for almost 90% of the time until the eggs hatch. The female loses her belly feathers and develops a 'brood patch' of bare skin for warming the eggs. This, stimulated by the contact with the smooth surface of the eggs, in turn develops an enlarged system of surface veins which act as a heat exchanger between the hen and the eggs. The male does not develop a true brood patch and undertakes less of the incubation (and in shorter bouts). Unlike many species he does not provide much food for the incubating hen and so she must leave the nest at regular intervals to feed.

Breeding takes place over quite a long period. Clutches, often in the same nest, may be started until the end of July and even into August in some years. Individual pairs sometimes have four broods in a season but the average is just over two – pairs with an inexperienced female will normally try fewer times (and also start, on average, two or three weeks later). If a breeding attempt fails through predation at the egg or nestling stage, replacement clutches will be laid very rapidly but often at a new site – it would be very imprudent for the birds to entrust their new attempt to a nest that had already been found by a predator and spoiled. The succession of tiny chicks found under Squeaker's parent's nest probably shows that they were therefore *not* the result of a predator's activities.

Since incubation started before the last eggs were laid hatching generally takes place over a period of 2 days or so. This will be between 9 days and 2½ weeks after the completion of the clutch. The average is about 12 days and appears to decrease slightly as the season progresses – possibly because the weather gets warmer. Hatching is an amazing process, for the naked chick has to batter its way out of the shell in which it has developed. The egg tooth, a sharp white excrescence, grows on the top of the upper mandible and is used to perforate the shell round the blunt end. The chick is eventually able to kick itself free (sometimes apparently helped by the female) and is hatch-ed. The female removes the eggshells from the nest as the chicks hatch – in doing so, it is possible that some chicks are chucked out too: was this Squeaker's problem? Could mother have been daft enough to have done this time after time? Probably not, but Squeaker certainly seems to have been less than 48 hours old when he made his first forlorn and enforced flight – down to the terrace.

The shrivelled yolk sac is still attached to the baby bird when it hatches and it does not necessarily need food straight away. At this stage heat is very important for the developing chicks and they are almost continuously brooded by one or other of their parents for the first 4 or 5 days. However, as Squeaker and E.T. showed, even the tiniest young are able to close down their metabolism and become cold and torpid and still survive. Some brooding continues during the rest of their first week but, after that, they have developed enough to be able to keep themselves warm in the relative shelter of the well-insulated nest.

Initially the chicks are fed by the parent regurgitating partly processed food items from the crop. This makes it difficult to see exactly what is being fed but direct observations show that the food for the first two or three days is almost all insects. Loraine did exactly the right thing with greenfly but she was probably better at getting froghoppers than parent sparrows are – the froth is an anti-bird device. Gradually the insect items become bigger – up to dismembered cockchafer – and the chicks are weaned from a very largely animal diet and start to receive the sort of vegetable food which the adults themselves usually take. This may be weed seeds or grain but is most likely to be bread from bird tables in many areas. Parent birds seem to be able to give their chicks a balanced diet by instinct but humans have to work hard at it.

One hesitates to recommend a baby sparrow diet in case young sparrows start to be reared all over Britain. However Les

Stocker, to whom I always turn for advice on such matters, suggests mashed up hard-boiled egg and chick-starter-pellets as the artificial food to use – if you are unable to find natural items in enough bulk for the voracious chick. It is very important to get this moist and crumbly so that it does not dehydrate the chick or make it messy by plastering glutinous food all over its plumage. Loraine had a close shave with Squeaker when she realized that solidifying food was bunging up his nostrils and they, of course, must be kept clear. The refinement of adding mealworms, a trace of cod-liver oil or dried terrapin food (moistened, of course) may be a little expensive but, once you have made the commitment to the bird, well worthwhile.

At the natural nest the parents will bring more beakfuls of food per hour in the early morning than during the afternoon. To start with the tiny insects fed to the day-old young may even be partly digested and regurgitated for the chicks. Soon, however, larger insects are brought whole to the nest and the parents may appear to grow dangling green moustaches if they find a good source of caterpillars. When seeds are being fed to the young they may be stored in the crop for the short flight to the nest but there will, of course, be no time for any pre-digestion to take place before the hungry young are fed and the next load needs to be collected. The number of feeds per day gradually increases until, when the young are about a week old, it will peak at more than 30 per hour in the morning, dropping gradually to 5 to 8 during the afternoon. The total will reach 300 or more per day, at this time, and all this material will either go into the fabric of the growing chicks or come out at the other end. Nest sanitation is vital and the parents eat the faeces of small chicks. They are stimulated to defaecate by the parents, after they have been fed, and do not do it at will in the nest. Later the faecal sacs, nicely parcelled up in a gelatinous membrane if the food is right, are taken out by the parents and dropped away from the nest. It was a good indication of Loraine's success that she had no problems with loose messy droppings from her brood. By the time the young are three-quarters grown they are squirting out of the nest entrance – an unappealing habit.

Loraine has described the development of Squeaker through this period and all sparrows will have gone through the same stages from naked chick to feathered bird. At between 13 and 17 days, on average, they will start to fledge. They are usually quite strong on the wing and immediately are looked after by their parents. If some are better developed than others the early ones fledge first and will be looked after by one parent whilst the other continues to tend the chicks that remain in the nest. At this stage the hopeful youngsters will solicit any sparrow they come across for food and may be lucky and get a response. This probably explains the activity of the Gang of Four in feeding Partlet.

In many species, especially in the tropics, related birds help a breeding pair during the breeding season. This has not been reported for house sparrows and, given their behaviour pattern, does not seem likely. However, it is quite possible that the social structure within the colony means that birds within it are sufficiently closely related for it to be beneficial for non-breeding birds to help feed fledglings out of the nest. The young cannot start to feed themselves for several days and will still be fed by their parents ten days to a fortnight after fledging.

With the house sparrow, as with other birds, the 'loyalty' shown by the parents to their nest, eggs and young steadily increases through the breeding cycle. This has a good ecological basis, for the parents have spent more and more time and energy in trying to rear the young the further on in the breeding cycle they have got. Indeed, by the time the fledged chicks have left the nest, the nesting attempt has occupied the parents full time for about five weeks (or the devoted and put-upon humans rather longer). It will also represent, on average, one of only two chances of rearing young during the season.

It is thus not surprising that the parents will often show what, to the human way of thinking, seems to be selfless devotion to their chicks, but is actually prudent protection of their investment of time and energy. It has come about by natural selection, for parents that look after their young better are more likely to have their genes passed on to future generations. This even shows in the normal feeding behaviour at an occupied nest when sparrows that will not normally come close, whilst one is watching, will come to feed the chicks only a few feet away. Several cases have been reported of parent birds feeding young in nests which have fallen down or even been pulled out and thrown away on a rubbish heap. Youngsters that have become trapped behind netting or a grille have sometimes been fed for days, even weeks, after they should have been able to fledge.

Perhaps the most remarkable case was reported many years ago by Yarrell of a pair at Poole, Dorset. They nested in a thatched roof and continued to make regular visits for a long time after the chicks should all have fledged. When this persisted into the winter a ladder was put up to the roof and it was discovered that a young sparrow had been caught in string used in lining the nest. It had been kept alive for months by its 'devoted' parents. Such hazards in the nest are not unusual and mummified corpses, attached to the nesting material, of adults and chicks are quite regularly reported. In one macabre case the chick became attached by string to the hen bird and so inconvenienced her that she was killed by a dog.

Some seven weeks after the previous one began, the parents are likely to start their next clutch. Obviously individual pairs that manage to have four broods in a year must start early and end late but also have to compress their efforts. This they can do by having the female start to lay the next clutch whilst the earlier brood are still dependent on their parents for food. In such a case the male will have to take more than his usual share of looking after the children but, of course, they have his genes in them and so this is a 'good thing'.

And So Into the Outside World

Unlike most newly fledged young birds, the sparrow chick (both species) faces a full moult not only of body feathers but also wings and tail. Most other species only replace the body feathers and keep the wings and tail that grew in the nest until autumn of the year after fledging. Other species in Britain with a full post-juvenile moult include the starling, corn bunting, both species of lark, long-tailed tit and all the woodpeckers. It may be that the sparrow chicks do not receive enough quality food to enable them to grow good, strong flight feathers in the nest. Certainly they often seem to be pretty poor in quality and would not have much chance of lasting through the wear and tear of a whole year. As with many species, the juvenile body feathers, which are only for use during the relatively mild summer and early autumn weather, are much sparser than the replacement ones.

From day ten Loraine noticed Squeaker preening. This is important for the nestlings since their new feathers emerge in a neat parchment-like package and this has to be got off where it clings to the base of the feather. Feathers are very intricate structures and they can easily get into disarray. The hooks on the individual vanes can be made to reconnect by the bird drawing them gently through its beak. Preening is very necessary for both the main flight feathers – their aerodynamics would soon be upset if they were not kept spruced up – and also for the body feathers which would let heat out and wet in.

House sparrows are inveterate bathers. They will use water – even what looks to us like filthy puddles – or dust. If both are available it is water first followed by dust. They can become very wet and bedraggled and often many birds from the flock will join one another at a favourite bathing place – generally where there is a reasonable view all round so that they will not be surprised by the sudden arrival of a predator. Perhaps surprisingly to the human way of looking at things, water bathing will take place even in the coldest weather – obviously impossible if the water is frozen – but during cold weather it is particularly important for the birds to have their plumage in top nick. Dry earth, sand, gravel by the road or even the path between the cabbages will do for dusting – Squeaker used the sand until Loraine had to empty it when she found the horrid evidence of a cat using the bath for other purposes. These activities are also designed to keep the plumage in good condition – and most do not have a human slave on whose hair they are able to dry themselves.

House sparrows also sunbathe a lot. Like all their activities this may be done communally and it can take place even in the depths of winter if the sun is out and the birds can find a suitably sheltered spot. Anyone can see that they luxuriate in it – pressed flat to the warm earth or a tiled roof with their wings outstretched. Summers-Smith watched one in 'this blissful state' for thirty minutes.

The newly independent youngsters will form into a flock with the products of the other nests in the colony and any adults that have finished breeding. In the past these flocks used regularly to leave the natal area and exploit corn crops in the open countryside. This still happens to a certain extent but the changes in agricultural practice over the last couple of decades have made a great difference to sparrow economics. The harvest is much earlier, as early maturing varieties of grain are grown, the combines are able to take wetter crops (which are then artificially dried) than in the past, and usually the stubble is immediately ploughed and sown; often after being burnt. This means that the period of the ripening crops during August, and stubble, with excellent feeding opportunities, in September and early October have vanished from many areas.

It seems therefore that many of the flocks of sparrows remain in the breeding area throughout the year. By the middle of August most of the young birds (and adults) will be well into their moult. This is the period when a delighted Loraine found that Squeaker was going to be a male because the first of the black feathers of his bib were grown. Some people think they can tell juvenile cocks and hens apart through slight plumage differences but this is very tricky – if indeed at all possible. However, as soon as the first new bib feathers have grown the girls can be sorted from the boys. The main flight feathers grow from the middle of the wing outwards to start with (primaries being moulted) and then, when the inner feathers of the outer half of the wing are fully grown, the other half of the wing starts to moult inwards. This regular pattern ensures that the birds do not have two adjacent parts of the wing in moult at the same time – this would impede their powers of flight.

The moult takes about seven or eight weeks to complete and many have finished by the end of September – virtually all by the end of October. Detailed analysis of the moulting regime of ringed birds shows that the very earliest youngsters to fledge may start their moult in June and spend up to 11 weeks completing it – after all, there is little else for them to do. Late youngsters, on the other hand, may not be able to start until mid-September – shortly after they have fledged. These birds rush through the feather replacement in as little as 7 weeks. Moult is very important for the bird's survival as they need the extra insulation of the new body feathers to keep them warm in the winter – the adult's old ones will be very worn. They also need the new flight feathers to make sure that they are as efficient as possible in the air; the adults suffer particularly badly and the outer primaries may have large areas of the tips broken off. Any feathers accidentally lost at other times of the year will be replaced – one of the main primaries takes about 12 weeks to grow.

At this stage the feeding birds will form a dense scrum where they can find a good food supply. This may be deliberately put out for bird feeding in the garden, spilt grain beside the road, food put out for farm stock or natural weed seeds on rough ground or along the banks of a reservoir – where the water level has dropped during the summer. All sorts of foods are eaten – but with all the familiar wariness, the birds often being very difficult to approach and watch. Even though the old-time food bonanza of the stubble is not generally available, this is a time of plenty and also of long days so the birds have many hours of light during which to feed. There is some evidence that the birds may even instinctively select particular weed seeds which contain the material needed for them to build new feathers – the protein from which they are made is synthesized by the birds from sulphur-based amino-acids which are not particularly common in much of the food the house sparrow eats. So it is not simply a case of the gluttonous sparrow always shovelling in the easiest foods it can find.

The feeding flocks have several advantages for the birds in them. They enable information to be shared about where good food supplies are – see some of your friends feeding and you can join them to share the food. The birds in the flock are all on the alert – sometimes it seems that individuals are designated as sentries – and so danger is likely to be spotted much earlier than if there were just an individual feeding by itself. The birds are also almost certainly finding out a lot about each other, for they are quite likely to be spending their lives together in the colony.

At night the flocks generally go to roost in relatively thick cover. Thorn bushes, rhododendrons and fir trees are often used and a real favourite is in the ivy on a wall or old tree. The roosting site is often advertised by the flocks when they arrive by flying around calling for a few minutes. Quite regularly roosting birds will arrive up to an hour 'early': that is, before the last ones arrive. The birds are usually very noisy as they jockey for position within the roost. The best places to hole up for the night are the most sheltered ones and generally those highest up – most danger in the night is likely to come from the ground in the form of climbing mammals. In some towns the roosts may be in bare trees or on (or even in) buildings. Very often the site chosen will be a traditional one which has held roosts for years and years. When large flocks formed on stubble the roosts often contained hundreds, even thousands, of birds, but such large ones are not common now. In a suburban area on the edge of farmland 200 or 300 birds is a good-sized roost and the colony roosts within a town might number less than 100.

During the day the sparrow flocks often spend quite a lot of time mooching about and not being very active. The birds usually gather at a favourite spot and will be well aware of what is happening around and about – although individuals may apparently nod off. The sort of sites used are in relatively open bushes, along window sills or ledges of buildings or even inside a barn or warehouse. Obviously Squeaker had a particular attachment to the rhododendrons.

As the birds come through their moult, in October and November, there is often a renewal of sexual activity involving both the adults and, as has been proved by colour-ringed individuals, some of the young birds of the year. Communal sexual chases are often seen and copulation may sometimes take place. This hardly ever – save in exceptional years – leads to any real nesting attempts and the meaning of the behaviour is unclear. However the genus *Passer* is undoubtedly of tropical origin and it is just possible that this may be a throwback to a twice yearly breeding cycle in a time when they lived where there were two rainy periods each year.

By the time winter has arrived the sparrows are experiencing really cold weather, long nights and short days. At the same time the natural food resources are being used up by all the species that feed on them. The house sparrow is in a much better position than other birds which are not prepared to accept or take from man. Bird tables are the obvious source but the resourceful sparrow will very often take even what is not offered. Birds regularly enter and feed in factory buildings, warehouses, grain-stores, stations, etc. Many of the birds will still be roosting communally, but some will have taken to spending the night in the nests they will be using next spring, as Loraine discovered, to her relief, during Squeaker's first winter.

By the time the days start to lengthen, at the end of December, many of the males will have established their nesting sites and some will already be paired. Often the weather gets worse at the beginning of the year but the lengthening days make survival that little bit easier day by day. The day-length also has its effect on the bird's physiology and so the breeding cycle is starting again. Sexual chases enliven the colony and the nest-building birds will start to quarrel over material and feathers. A new clutch of eggs is on its way in each nest. And so the story starts anew.